Maps Are Cool!

How to Read Them, Plan Them, and Create Them

By John Tauranac

MONDO

My sincere thanks to Peter Joseph for his technical savvy;
Amy Cady of the Cornwall, Connecticut, library for her able assistance;
and, of course, my family for everything else that is good.

Text and maps copyright ©2007 by John Tauranac
under exclusive license to Mondo Publishing
Map p. 4: cr. Maggie Tauranac
All rights reserved.

For information contact:
Mondo Publishing
980 Avenue of the Americas
New York, NY 10018
Visit our website at www.mondopub.com

Printed in China

07 08 09   9 8 7 6 5 4 3 2 1
ISBN 1-59336-718-X

Interior design by John Tauranac and Peter Joseph
Cover design by Witz End Design

Contents

Introduction

What Makes a Good Map?

Let me tell you something that you will probably find a little odd. I am a mapmaker by trade. And for my money, maps that are drawn on the backs of envelopes, or maps that show you where to find a pirate's buried treasure, are often about as good as maps can get. That's because they usually do exactly what a map is supposed to do.

A good map does three things: 1) shows you where you are, 2) shows you where places are in relation to each other, and 3) shows you how to get where you want to go. A good map shows only information that is important and relevant—information that is critical to navigation. If a map is beautiful but doesn't get you where you want to go, it fails. Look at this map that was hastily drawn on the back of an envelope. The map works. It's easy to see what you need to know to get to the movies from where you are:

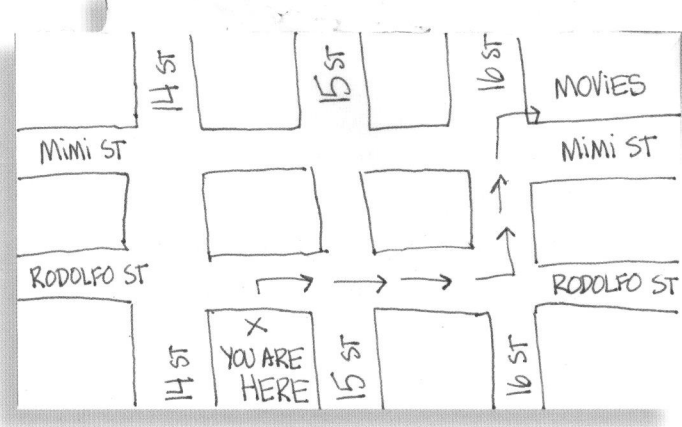

1. Turn right when you leave the house.
2. Cross one street.
3. Turn left at the second street.
4. Walk another block, cross another street, and there you are.

Mapmaking Is a Process

Let's say you want to make a map of your neighborhood. You probably already have a lot of information in your head. But you should still go out and scout because you probably don't know exactly where everything is. When you think you have enough information, you can start laying out the map. Then you can make decisions about what to keep and what to leave out.

Unless you are designing a map that is meant to show where all your relatives live, don't show Cousin Minnie's house just because it is there. You don't want to confuse people with too much information. Maps need editing, just as writing does. In fact, the process of creating a good map is a lot like the writing process.

1. Plan: decide the purpose and content of your map. Who will use the map? What will they use it for? Decide on the information they will need. Refer back to your plan over and over as you work.

2. Compose: gather information and organize it according to your plan. For example, on a neighborhood map, what landmarks will be important? What streets are they on? Do you need to check street names? Which way is north?

3. Record: make your rough draft. Sketch things in where you think they will go. Plot important information. Is there too much? Is something missing?

4. Edit: make another draft or work in a computer drawing program. Clarify things that are confusing. Add information that's important and take out what isn't. Always keep your purpose and audience in mind.

5. Publish: create the final map, either carefully by hand with colored pencils or on the computer.

A map should be as geographically accurate as possible, or at least it should appear to be. If the blocks in our little map were depicted in true scale, they would be much larger. As a result, the streets would be narrower in order to fit everything on the envelope. If the streets were narrower, their names might not fit. There is always some give and take. But the map *appears* accurate.

If you are making a highway map, your job is to show roads in relation to the land; to other roads; and to cities, towns, parks, rivers, and so on. On paper, the roads will be larger in relation to the land than they really are. If the roads were shown in true scale, they would be far too small to see. Readers will understand.

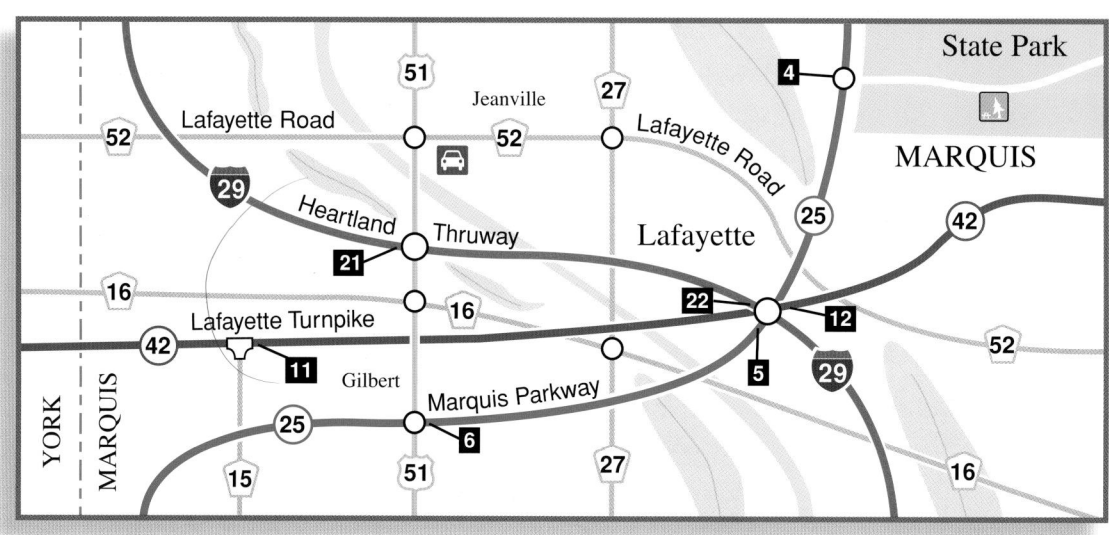

A map should be neat and easy to read.

A map doesn't necessarily have to be pretty, but it does have to be neat. A messy or cluttered map is hard to read and even harder to understand and use. If readers can't understand a map, they won't use it.

The Buried Treasure Map

Back to the pirate map. A good pirate's buried treasure map usually shows specific landmarks that help you get your bearings and orient yourself. "To get your bearings" is a nautical term that means "to figure out your relative position, or learn where you are." "To orient yourself" refers to a tradition used by mapmakers in the Middle Ages. They put the East, or the Orient, at the tops of their maps. ("We put the North" at the top of our maps, but we still say that we orient ourselves.)

On page 8 is a pirate's buried treasure map that is really two maps in one. It shows both the overall land and a detail of where the treasure will be found. We'll assume that this is a real map, drawn by a real pirate. Some people say that the pirate in question might never have buried his treasure in the first place. And if he had, he would probably have buried it hundreds of miles from where we show it. The pirate was Captain William Kidd.

Captain Kidd's map includes a compass rose. Some of the fancier ones have reminded people of the flower by that name. The compass rose, just like a real compass, points to the north, so you can orient yourself.

Captain Kidd's map also includes the exact spot in longitude and latitude, terms a sailor would understand. Longitude measures the distance east or west of an imaginary line drawn from the North Pole to the South Pole. It is called the *meridian*, and is centered at Greenwich, England. Latitude measures the distance north or south of the Equator, another imaginary line around the earth midway between the two poles.

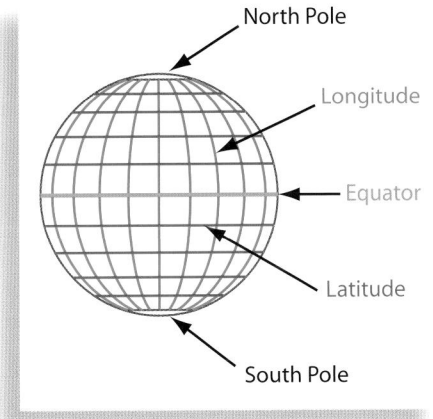

There is a scale that shows the distance, and it even tells you the amount of time it should take to row from his house on Pearl Street to Turtle Bay, where the treasure is buried. So if you've been rowing for two or three hours, and Captain Kidd has told you that the trip should take about 40 minutes with the tide, you might want to turn around.

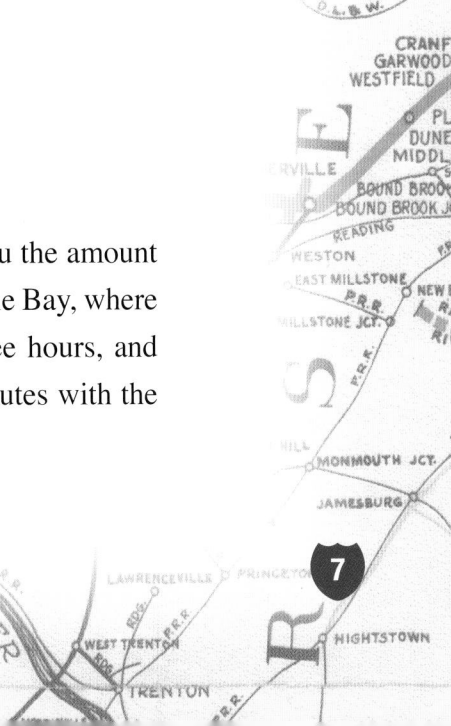

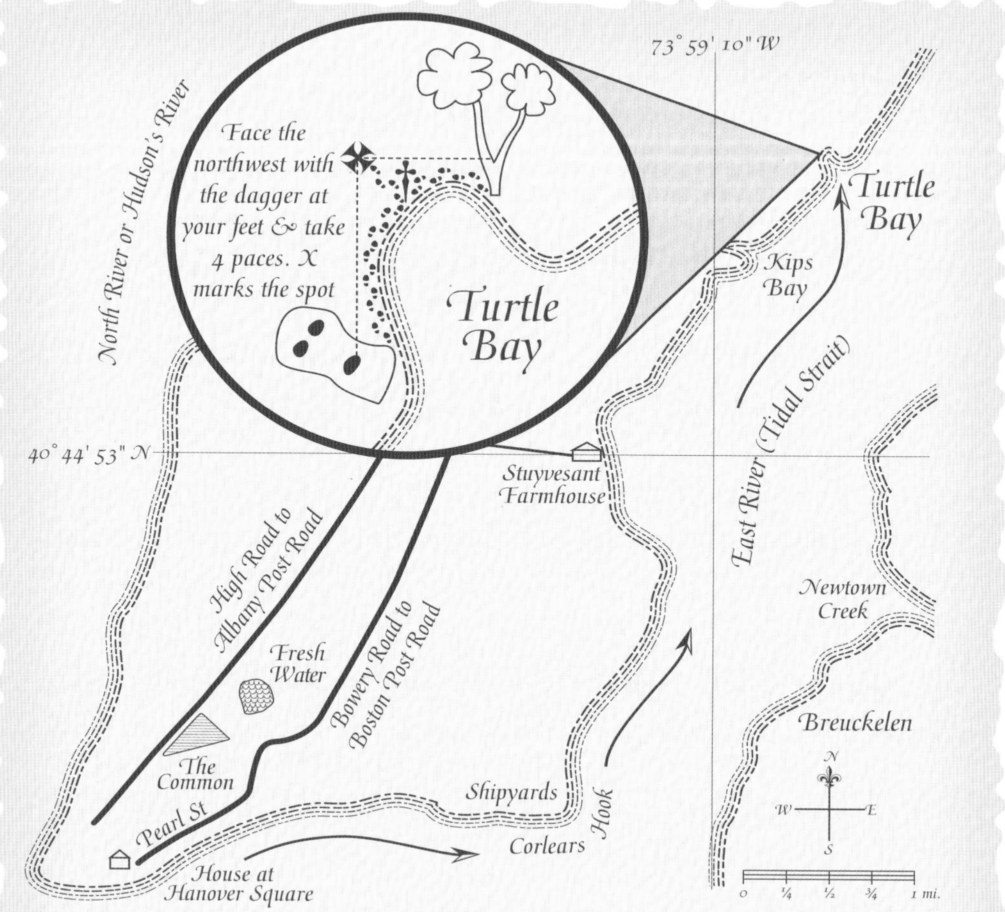

Face the northwest with the dagger at your feet & take 4 paces. X marks the spot

73° 59' 10" W

North River or Hudson's River

40° 44' 53" N

Turtle Bay

Turtle Bay

Kips Bay

Stuyvesant Farmhouse

East River (Tidal Strait)

High Road to Albany Post Road

Bowery Road to Boston Post Road

Fresh Water

The Common

Pearl St

Shipyards

Corlears Hook

House at Hanover Square

Newtown Creek

Breuckelen

N
W — E
S

0   ¼   ½   ¾   1 mi.

From my house on Pearl Street at Hanover Square, row with the tide on the East River due east to Corlears Hook, then northward for about 40 minutes until you come to Turtle Bay. Beach your craft and look for a two-headed white birch and the rock like a Jolly Roger head. Pace off 7 steps from the birch tree along the beach on a westerly line, and mark the spot with your dagger. Then take 13 paces from the rock on a northerly line. You should arrive at the same spot. Then pace off 4 steps northwest. X marks the spot. To be perfectly sure, take out your spyglass. Look east. You should be on a line with the fork in the tree. Then look south to see Jolly Roger's mouth. May it smile on you.

Helpful as it is, however, Captain Kidd's map has one major flaw. Although you see several names, a critical place name is missing. It is the name of the island—Manhattan, the heart of New York City.

Captain Kidd lived in New York in the early 1690s at what the best sources believe is now 119 Pearl Street. On our map, Captain Kidd assumed that you would understand that the land in question is Manhattan. But you should never assume anything in mapmaking. Always show the obvious.

Landfill now covers Turtle Bay on the East River at what is now 46th Street and First Avenue. The United Nations stands nearby, closer to the river than the cove would have been. Captain Kidd's house on Pearl Street is also long gone. An office building now stands on the site.

The Bowery was the road that led to Peter Stuyvesant's farm, and his farmhouse could be easily seen from the East River, which made it a good landmark for anyone rowing up the river.

Captain Kidd's treasure, if it was buried anywhere, has never been dug up. At least, not that we know.

1 Starting Small: Floor Plans

Practice With Familiar Places

When you think of making a map, maybe you think of exploring uncharted territory the way Lewis and Clark did. The goal of this book is not to turn you into an explorer, a surveyor, or even a cartographer, although any of those careers would be interesting and fun. The goal is for you to understand the stories that maps can tell, to show you how to read a map, and to show you how you can create your own. To do that, I'm first going to have you "write" a map. That way you will understand what goes into a map. You'll work with two small areas that are probably fairly familiar: a library and a swimming pool.

Let's not even call these maps. Maps are geographic pictures of large places drawn small. They can be drawn so small that you can have the map of the entire world on one page. Let's call what you are going to do plans, because we are really talking about floor plans. Compared to maps, floor plans are fairly large-scale drawings of rather small places, such as rooms. We are not talking about mapping Texas. Since I don't know the shape or dimensions of what you are going to chart, I will simply provide a model that you can follow.

The Tools of the Trade

You will need some tools. Some are for measuring, others for drawing. If you have computer software with a simple drawing program, you might want to use it for the finished product instead of some of the tools in this list.

1. Magnetic Compass

The first thing that you need is a magnetic compass—the kind that has a magnetic attraction to the North Pole. You might think it's strange that you need a compass when you are only trying to find the dimensions of a room. But it's sometimes important to know which way the windows face, for instance.

2. Circle Compass

A circle compass is a tool for making circles of a particular size. You can also use one for drawing round tables on a floor plan, or to draw an arc (part of a circle) to show the swing of a door on a floor plan.

3. Carpenter's Tape Measure

For measuring things like rooms, a carpenter's tape measure is ideal. Just pull the tab and out comes a metal ruler that will extend as far as 25 or 30 feet (7.6–9 m). Measuring long distances may require two people—one to hold the end of the tape at the starting point and the other to walk to the end point while stretching out the tape. Keeping the tape taut along the floor ensures that it will be straight. As you make your measurements, jot them down. The average room is a rectangle, but you also need to note things like closets and windows.

4. Paper, Pencils, Eraser

Make your notes and drawings with a pencil. You can use plain or lined paper for your early drafts, but it's usually easier to use graph paper, which is divided into little squares. Let each square equal a unit, such as a foot or three meters or 100 feet. You will no doubt find yourself revising your original drawing, or rough draft. Then you will probably revise it again, and then again. A good artist's eraser will come in handy. Kneaded erasers can be shaped to erase fine lines. They are clean and don't make a lot of crumbs.

5. T-square, Triangle, Ruler

A T-square pretty much describes itself. It is a ruler in the shape of a T. The T-square is designed so that you can place the top of the T along the edge of a table or a pad of paper. The straight edge extends across your paper. This allows you to draw a series of straight lines that are perfectly parallel. Use one for your final drawing. You may find it convenient to have a separate 12-inch (30 cm) ruler as well.

A triangle is another drafting tool that looks the way it sounds. It is a piece of clear or tinted plastic in the shape of a right triangle. Triangles come in several sizes. If you want to draw a perfect right angle or a vertical line that is perpendicular to a line you drew with your T-square, just place the base of the triangle along the edge of the T-square and draw your line.

6. Colored Pencils

Once you have outlined everything on your final draft and are ready to add some color, use colored pencils. Color can be very helpful in making certain objects stand out, for showing the depth or height of something, and for making it easy to tell the land from the water. With pencils, you can use pressure to make the color deeper or lighter, and you can erase—something you can't do with markers or crayons.

7. Computer + Software

If you have computer software with a drawing program, such as Microsoft Word®, try using it to make your final drawing. With a computer, you can measure objects accurately, and make perfect circles and squares and everything in between. You can also use color to fill in or for outlines, making your drawing look quite professional. A computer was used for almost all the plans and maps in this book, but people were making maps long before there were any computers. You can make any kind of map you wish just as well by hand as by computer.

Making a Library Floor Plan

The first floor plan you might try is a library. You can use the library in your school or your local public library. But before you actually start charting, be sure to go to the librarian, explain what you want to do, and ask permission. With permission, you are ready to begin.

1. Look at the general shape of the library and see how things are arranged. Start by walking around the boundaries of the library. Hug the wall and note all the innies and outies, all the nooks and crannies. Note where the bookshelves are, where the desks and chairs are placed, and where the windows and doors are located.

2. Think about the scale you are going to use when you draw your plan. Obviously you can't make your plan the same size as the library. You have to make it smaller and it has to fit on your paper. Let's say you are going to have a scale of $\frac{1}{4}''$ = 1 foot. This means that something that is one foot or 12 inches long in real life is only $\frac{1}{4}$ inch long on your plan.

3. Start measuring the length of the walls, remembering to include doors and windows in their appropriate places. You can indicate windows with rectangles that look like this: ▭ .

Doors can be a straight line with an arc to indicate how the door swings.

4. Translate your measurements into the measurements you will use on your map. For example, if one wall is 22 feet long, it will be 22 x $\frac{1}{4}''$ or $5\frac{1}{2}''$ long on your plan.

5. When you come to things like bookshelves against the wall, measure the length of the bookcase. It will occupy that much wall space on your plan,

reduced according to your scale. On this plan, a 4-foot bookcase would be an inch long. If you like, measure the depth of the bookcase at the same time.

6. Start with a rough draft, or sketch. Draw the perimeter of the room first. Then add the doors and windows, then the bookshelves. Show reading tables and chairs. Draw and label the librarian's desk, the computers, and where you check out and return books.

7. It's a good idea to label what kinds of books are shelved where. For example, note where the reference books are shelved. Next find where fiction is kept. Then find biographies and other nonfiction categories. Assign a color to each of these primary subjects. If your library already color-codes its books by genre, use the same color-coding. There are only about a dozen colors that can be easily distinguished from one another. Since you are color-coding general subjects, you don't have to label them on the plan, but you should include the color-codes and the scale ($\frac{1}{4}'' = 1$ foot) in a key. Think of a key as something that unlocks the meaning of the symbols and colors. The scale tells people the size of what is on the paper in relation to its size in reality.

8. When you have completed your first draft, make a second, or even a third. Getting it right the first time is pretty unlikely. Revisions are always allowed, even encouraged. When the plan is neat and you are satisfied that everything is there and in correct relationship to everything else, you are ready to create your final draft, your finished plan.

9. Assemble your tools. If you are working by hand, in addition to paper and pencils, you will need a ruler or T-square, a triangle, and a circle compass when you start your final drawing. Bookshelves are usually rectangular, tables might be circles or squares or rectangles, chairs can be straight-fronted and round-backed, and so on.

10. In addition to your color-coded bookshelves, add color sparingly. All furniture, for instance, might be light brown.

11. Make a key and add a title.

Here is a small library for middle schoolers. A library that is 26 feet long and 22 feet wide plus the key might look like this. Remember that the final version of this plan was done on a computer. If yours is hand-drawn, it won't look quite the same, but it will be every bit as accurate and useful—and maybe even more attractive!

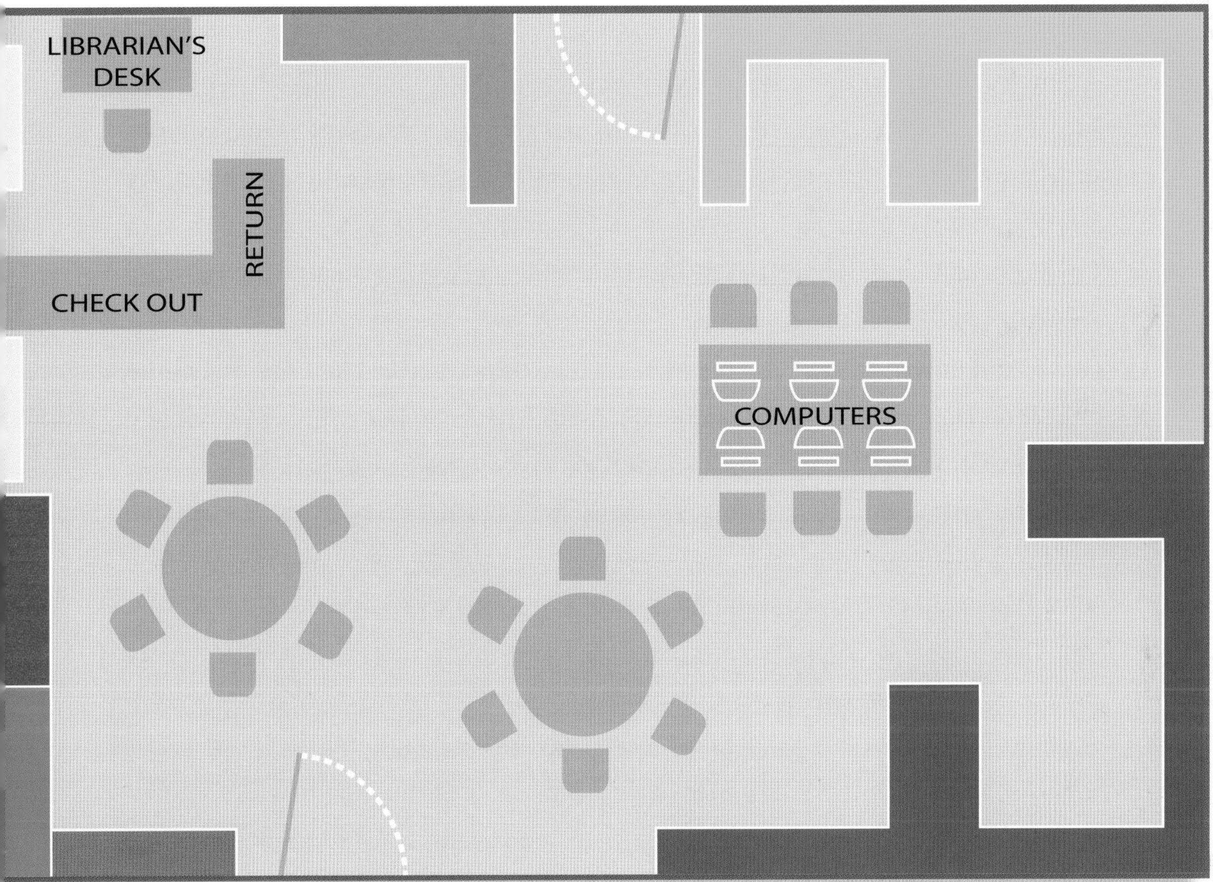

LIBRARIAN'S DESK

RETURN

CHECK OUT

COMPUTERS

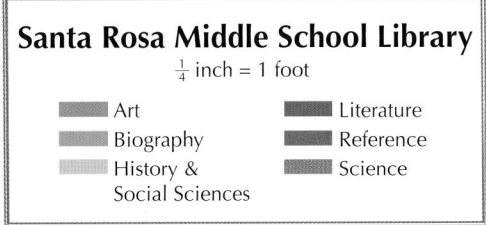

Santa Rosa Middle School Library

$\frac{1}{4}$ inch = 1 foot

- Art
- Biography
- History & Social Sciences
- Literature
- Reference
- Science

Making a Swimming Pool "Floor" Plan

Here's another way to use color. Gradations (different tints, from light to dark) of color can show how deep or shallow something is. You can chart a swimming pool and show the various depths of the water.

Water is traditionally blue on maps. The deeper the water, the deeper or darker the blue. If there is a public pool near you, pay a visit and note the depths indicated along the side of the pool. Let those depths be your guide. If your area has no public pools, you may have to visit a privately-owned pool (again, be sure to ask permission) and measure the depths of the water using a long pole. Just dip the pole into the water until it hits the bottom, mark where the water comes to on the pole, and measure from there to the end of the pole with your carpenter's tape measure. Do this four or five times from the shallow to the deep end and note your measurements.

We know that the bottoms of pools slope gradually. They don't go from four feet deep to eight feet deep in one drop. But don't worry about showing a complete gradation of colors. Just have the color change halfway between the two depths that you are showing, as we do in the example on page 17. Separate the depths with a white line.

The pool in the example shows five depths. At the ten-foot depth, we use the deepest blue to show the deepest water. At the eight-foot depth, we use a slightly lighter blue. At the six-foot depth, a still lighter blue, and so on. If you are using colored pencils, you can do this with just one pencil. Practice using pressure to create five shades of blue, dark to light.

10 Feet	
8 Feet	
6 Feet	
4 Feet	
2 Feet	

A key might be helpful, but you probably don't need one to show the depths. The colors do that for you, and you will also show the depths along the side of the pool.

Be sure to measure both the width and length of the pool. If it is a free-form pool, take measurements in several places, and draw the shape the best you can. You might also indicate ladders, diving boards, steps, doors leading to the changing rooms—anything that contributes to the overall picture and puts things in perspective.

If you want someone to meet you at one precise spot when you are finished with your plan, there is only one thing left to do. Add a note saying, "Meet me here!" and let **X** mark the spot. It might be right in the middle of the pool!

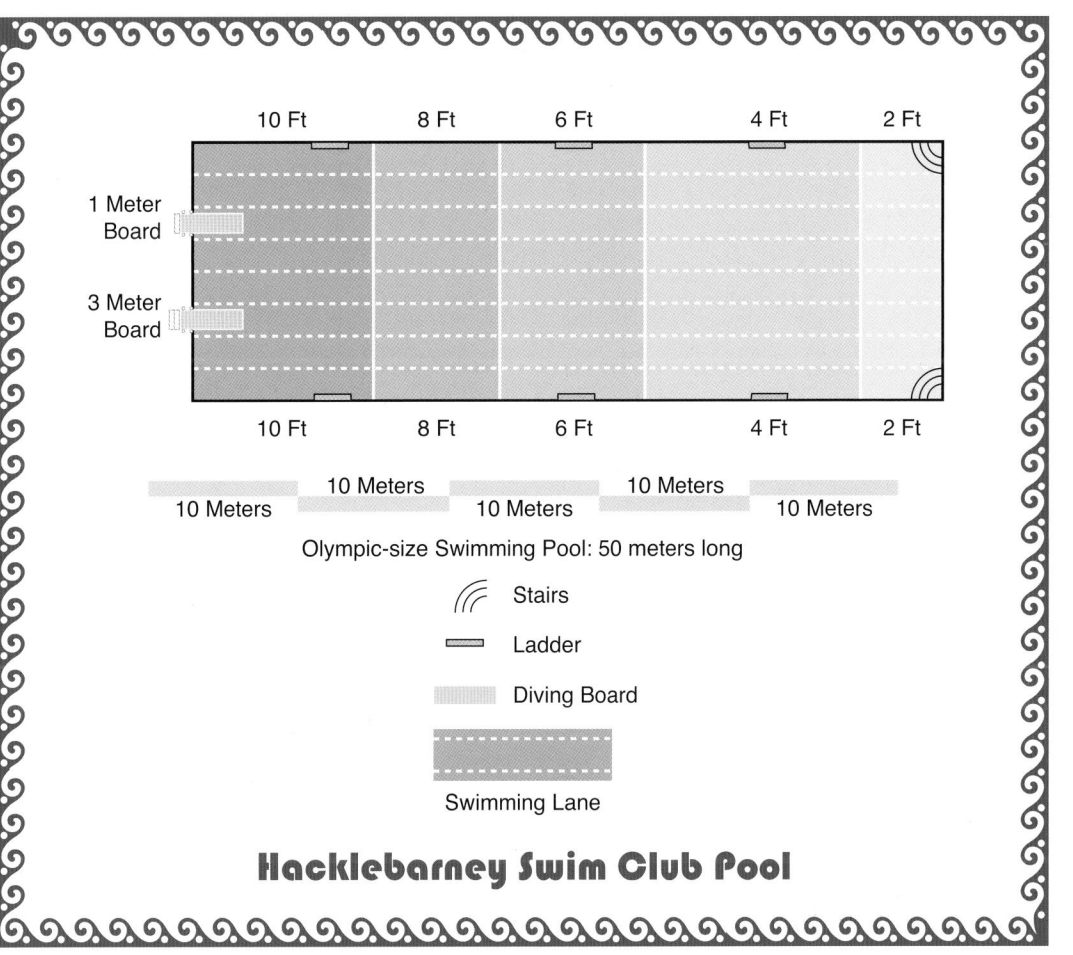

Hacklebarney Swim Club Pool

The Story of Bay City

You've seen how different shades of blue can indicate the depth of water in a swimming pool. Now think about how different shades of blue might show the depths of water in a bay, a river, or an ocean. Another set of colors can show how high the land rises. Now we are talking about a topographic map.

A topographic map shows natural features, such as rivers and mountains, and man-made places, such as cities and towns and reservoirs, and how they relate to each other. If the map is drawn correctly, it should not need many words other than place names.

The topographic map on page 19 shows an area of land in its natural state, before it was developed into a port city. It looks the way any number of places might have looked before they were settled and became towns and cities. We will call this peninsula and the neighboring land the future site of Bay City.

The Peninsula

The peninsula (A) was selected as a settlement for several reasons. The ocean is south of the narrow opening (B) that you see at the bottom. That narrow opening, which is called the Neck, serves as a breakwater, or wave breaker—it protects the harbor from the perils of stormy seas.

To the west of the peninsula is a river (C) that provides access to the interior of the land—a water route that would help trade develop and flourish to the north. The big river—as big a river as any of the settlers had ever seen—would be the lifeline between Bay City and the upstream farms and towns, such as one we will call Arborville.

A French settler called the river *Le Grand Fleuve*, French for "The Big River." A *fleuve* is not just any river—it is a river that flows into the sea. Non-French-speaking settlers had a tough time pronouncing *fleuve*, and called the river the Granflo. The name stuck.

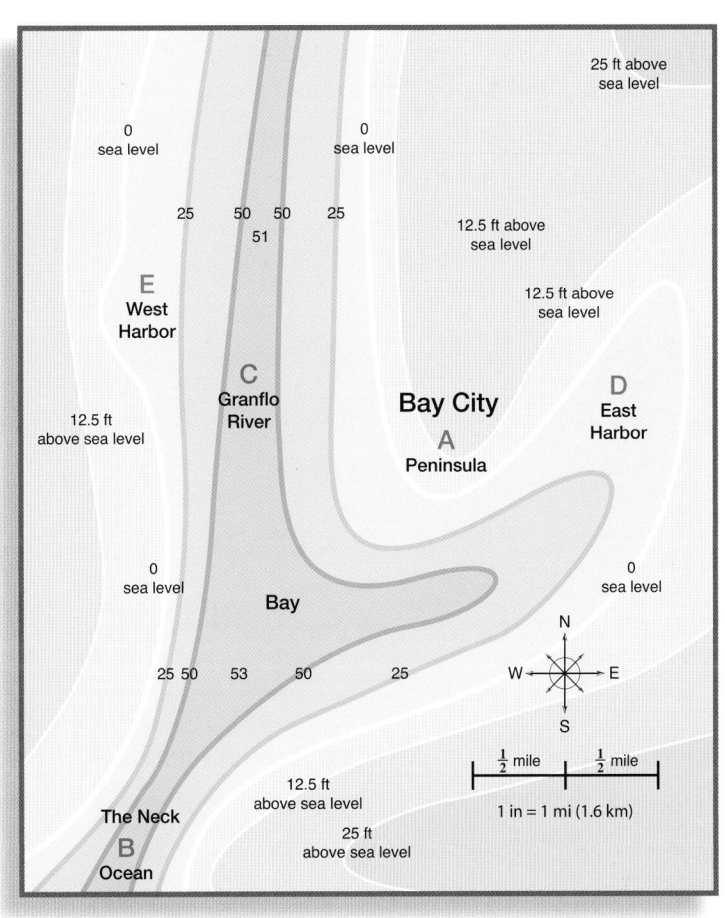

This map shows the basic topography of Bay City and environs.

To the east of the peninsula is a safe harbor (D) that is tidal. Ships had an easy time docking on incoming tides and sailing out on outgoing tides. The harbor was relatively free of the currents found in the big river. That harbor would serve the eastern shore of the peninsula.

The gently curving bay to the northwest (E) would serve as a harbor for the western shore. So important did that docking area become that when the region's first railroad opened in 1845, it would be the West Shore Railroad.

You see shades of blue to show the depths of water, just as you saw with the swimming pool plan. Here, the different depths are separated by blue outlines.

To show the varying heights of land, we have used shades of tan with white outlines. Numbers indicate depths and heights as well. If you draw a map like this by hand, first make the outlines and then fill in the colors. The key would look like this.

	Land 25–37.5 ft above sea level
	Land 12.5–25 ft above sea level
	Land 0–12.5 ft above sea level
	Water 0–25 ft deep
	Water 25–50 ft deep
	Water 50+ ft deep

The River

The map on page 21 shows the Granflo River from the place where it empties into the ocean at the Neck all the way upstream to a point about 28 miles north. This map needed a different scale because in the same amount of space in which we showed the future site of Bay City (about 4.5 miles north to south) we are now showing about 18 miles north to south. That means that each inch must represent more miles than it did on the last map. On the first map, one inch equalled one-half mile (.8 km). On this map, one inch equals 4 miles (6.4 km).

Look at the different shores. In general, the land on the eastern shore of the Granflo rose gently to 50 and 75 feet above sea level. One ridge stretched along at 100 feet. The ridge had a high point 123 feet above sea level, where there was a lake called Lake of the Clouds. Dancing Lake was to the southeast and was 119 feet above sea level. These lakes fed a fast-flowing river that dropped sharply as it flowed into the Granflo. It was about 22 miles north of Bay City.

The western shore of the Granflo was different. Here, dramatic cliffs lined the shore north of Bay City. Access to the interior was difficult except for one spot about eight miles upriver, where the land dipped down to meet the Granflo.

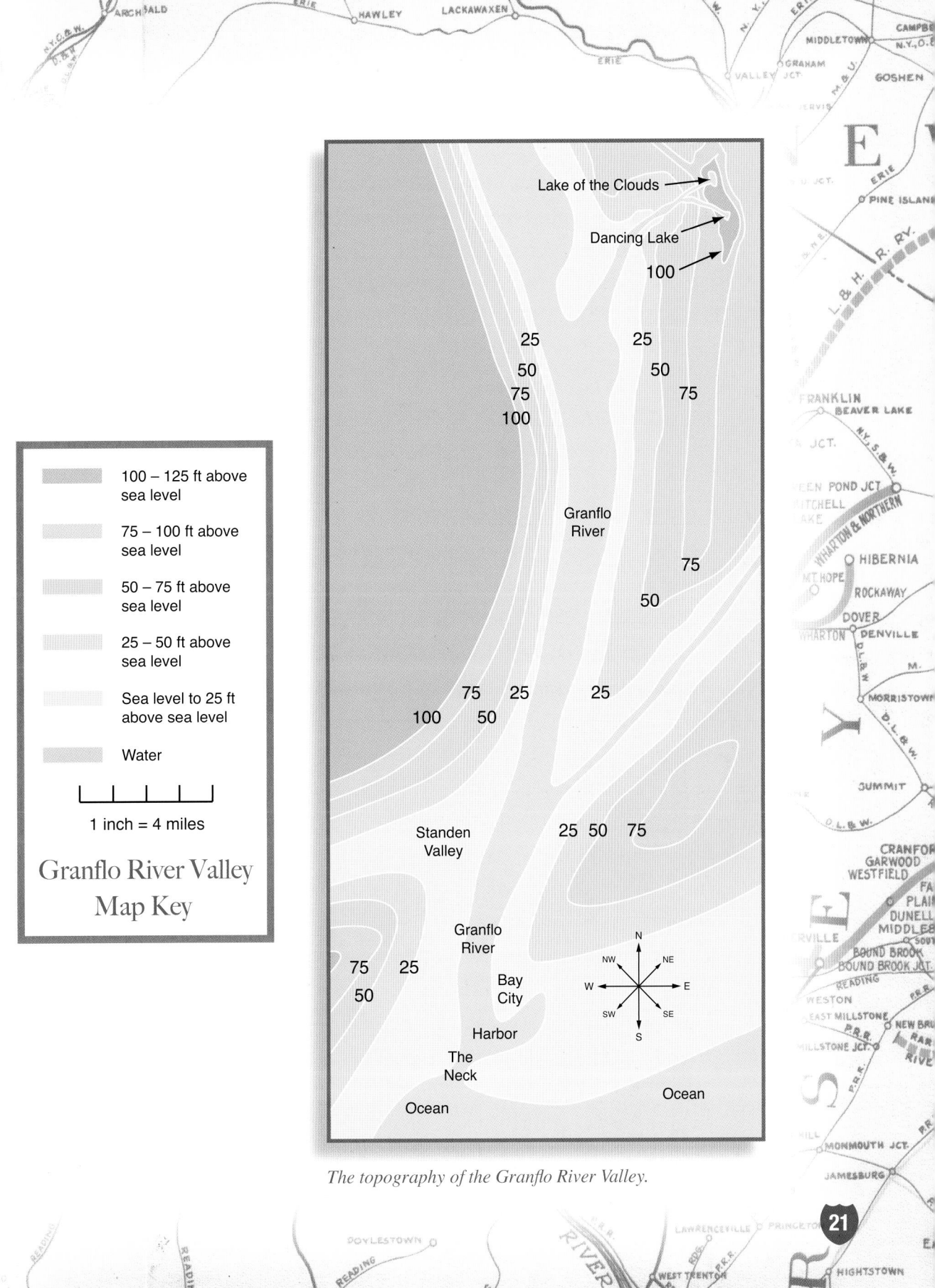

Granflo River Valley Map Key

	100 – 125 ft above sea level
	75 – 100 ft above sea level
	50 – 75 ft above sea level
	25 – 50 ft above sea level
	Sea level to 25 ft above sea level
	Water

1 inch = 4 miles

Lake of the Clouds

Dancing Lake

100

25   25
50   50
75   75
100

Granflo River

75

50

75   25   25
100   50

Standen Valley

25 50   75

Granflo River

75   25
50

Bay City

Harbor

The Neck

Ocean   Ocean

N
NW   NE
W   E
SW   SE
S

The topography of the Granflo River Valley.

This was the Standen Valley, which would become the main route west from Bay City. It was named for the Standen Inn, where travelers stopped for one last night in a featherbed before heading west. They took the same route that the West Shore Railroad would eventually follow.

You can make out the topography of the land with help from the color key. I've used the same shades as earlier. But since this is a different map, the colors represent different things.

Bay City's Streets

Bay City was first settled in the early 18th century. As it grew, its street patterns became more and more random. If cows beat down a path to reach the watering hole north of town, that cowpath might become a footpath, and the footpath would probably develop into a lane, and then into a street.

As Bay City's population grew, streets in one section of Old Town did not necessarily line up with streets of another. This was because most of the land north of the original settlement had once been farms. When the farmers started selling their property to developers (people who would put the land to new and different uses, mostly houses) the new housing developments followed the oddly-shaped property boundaries. And so did the streets.

By the mid-19th century, Bay City residents realized that they needed a plan for the development of their growing city. So the mayor appointed a committee to study the street plans in other cities. You can see the result of their new plan for Bay City in the map on page 23. It shows the old street patterns in one shade and the new in another. But you probably didn't need to be told that. The street patterns give it away.

The committee didn't try to deal with the part of the city that had already been developed. They just drew a line at the north end of the already-developed area and said, "This is where the new Bay City will begin."

The first thing that the committee decided was that there should be primary or main streets, and secondary streets. Main streets would be 100 feet wide, secondary streets would be 75 feet wide.

Portion of the Bay City Street Plan

The new streets in Bay City were straight and met at right angles except at traffic circles.

The committee agreed with the people running stores and other businesses that straight-sided, right-angled buildings were the most economical to build. They decided that the street plan should go along with that sensible building pattern, so all the streets are at right angles to each other.

The committee felt that public spaces like parks and squares are important. They decided that public squares would be placed where the 100-foot wide (30 m) or main streets crossed. To keep these areas quiet, the streets alongside the squares would be only 50 feet (15 m) wide. That meant that there would be one-way traffic on the streets around the squares. Horses would have to slow down, so there would probably be less noise and fewer accidents. Maybe the drivers of commercial horse-drawn wagons would even choose secondary streets to avoid having to slow down around a square. This would make the areas around the squares even nicer.

Traffic circles allow traffic to flow more freely. This appealed to store owners. So the city decided to place traffic circles in areas planned for business, arts, and civic centers. The circles would make the plan a bit more classy, and buildings such as city hall, the courthouse, and museums could be built around them. The committee figured that the city government would be happy to pay for all this classiness since it would polish up the city's image.

On a more practical level, deliveries had to be made and trash had to be hauled away. The solution was to have 20-foot wide (6 m) alleys running through the middle of most blocks.

All of this information is right there in the city street plan. Although you can't tell the widths of the streets, you can see that some are wider than others. You can also see that the narrowest streets (the alleys) are running through the middle of the blocks.

The map on page 26 is another version of the basic street map of Bay City. The same map, however, now tells another story. Here's what one newspaper headline said:

BAY CITY GAZETTE

AUGUST 2, 1859

ALL THE NEWS

VOLUME X, NUMBER 1

CONFLAGRATION!

TERRIBLE FIRE DESTROYS 56 BLOCKS

Headlines in Bay City's newspapers all announced the same news: A horse kicked over a kerosene lantern in a wood-framed warehouse. The resulting fire spread rapidly. Fueled by a breeze from the southeast, the flames leaped from one wooden building to another. Most of the buildings on 56 blocks of Old Town and in some of the city's new town were destroyed. Blocks that were totally or partially burned down are shown in gray, the color of ashes.

One reason that the fire spread so quickly was that firefighters couldn't get water fast enough. There was no water-delivery system, such as fire hydrants. When the fire pumpers were empty, volunteer firefighters had to go to a stream or to the Granflo for water. Then they had to race back through crowded streets to the scene of the fire. The layout of the streets in Old Town made rapid travel impossible. Drivers had to zig and zag because no streets provided a straight route to or from the fire. Using the streets that were part of the new plan actually made travel faster, even though the distance was greater.

But soon it was too late. Despite valiant efforts, the firefighters simply could not get enough water to the fire. The flames finally subsided when they could not make the leap across a new circle that was ringed by a 100-foot wide street. But even then, burning embers kept showering down on buildings, forcing the residents and volunteers to wet down the roofs.

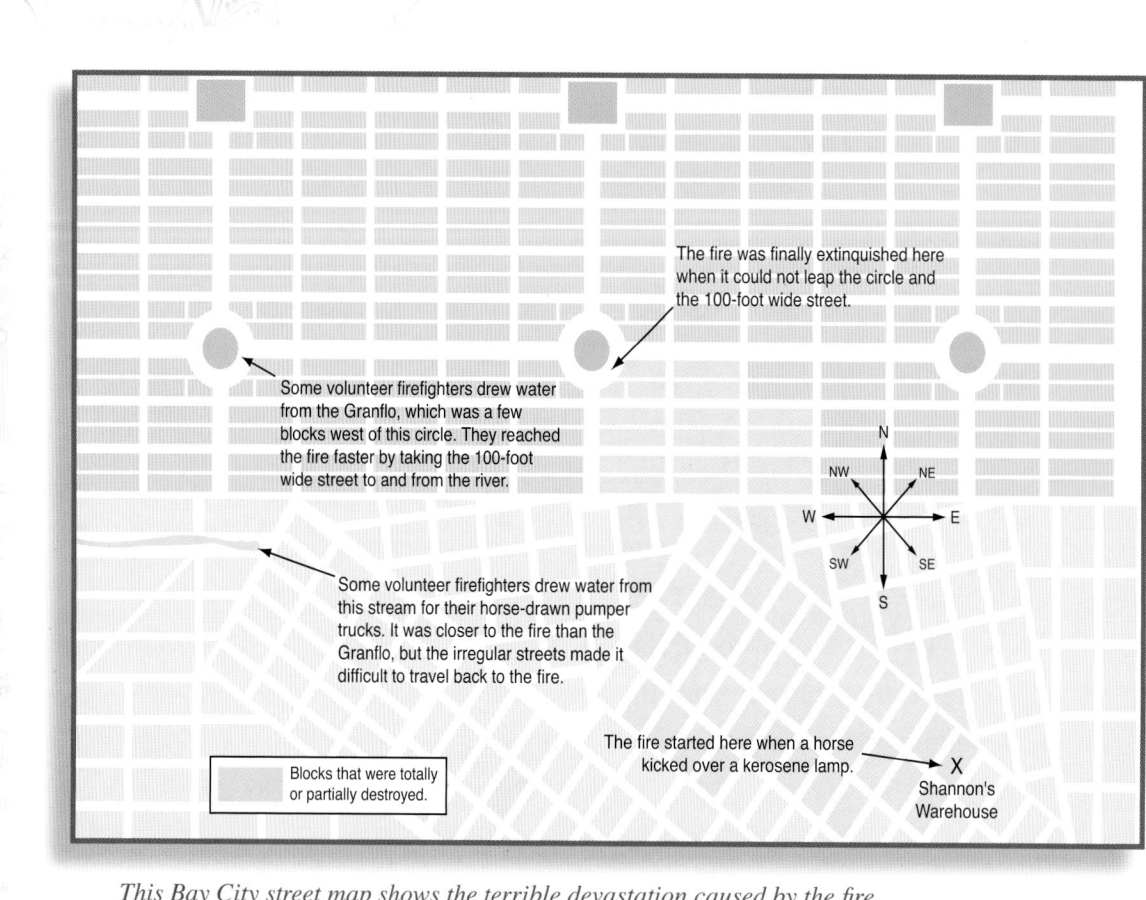

The fire was finally extinguished here when it could not leap the circle and the 100-foot wide street.

Some volunteer firefighters drew water from the Granflo, which was a few blocks west of this circle. They reached the fire faster by taking the 100-foot wide street to and from the river.

N
NW   NE
W   E
SW   SE
S

Some volunteer firefighters drew water from this stream for their horse-drawn pumper trucks. It was closer to the fire than the Granflo, but the irregular streets made it difficult to travel back to the fire.

The fire started here when a horse kicked over a kerosene lamp.

X
Shannon's Warehouse

Blocks that were totally or partially destroyed.

This Bay City street map shows the terrible devastation caused by the fire.

Several lessons were learned from the fire.

1. The new street pattern allowed emergency vehicles to reach the scene faster. Wide streets, circles, and squares served as firebreaks that helped prevent the spread of fire. Firefighters could also drive their pumpers into the alleys, thus adding to the streams of water that could be pumped onto the flames.

2. Wooden buildings had fed the fire. The mayor banned new construction of wooden buildings within the city limits. Builders had to use brick or stone, or some other fire-retardant material.

3. Bay City needed a dependable water-supply system. As people pointed out, water was important for more than just putting out fires. If Bay City was to be a modern city, it needed clean running water for drinking, bathing, street cleaning, and businesses. Bay City needed a reservoir.

The Story of Arborville

Arborville, or Treetown, was named in the early 19th century by a settler named Sawyer. True to his name, he wanted to operate a sawmill to supply lumber to Bay City.

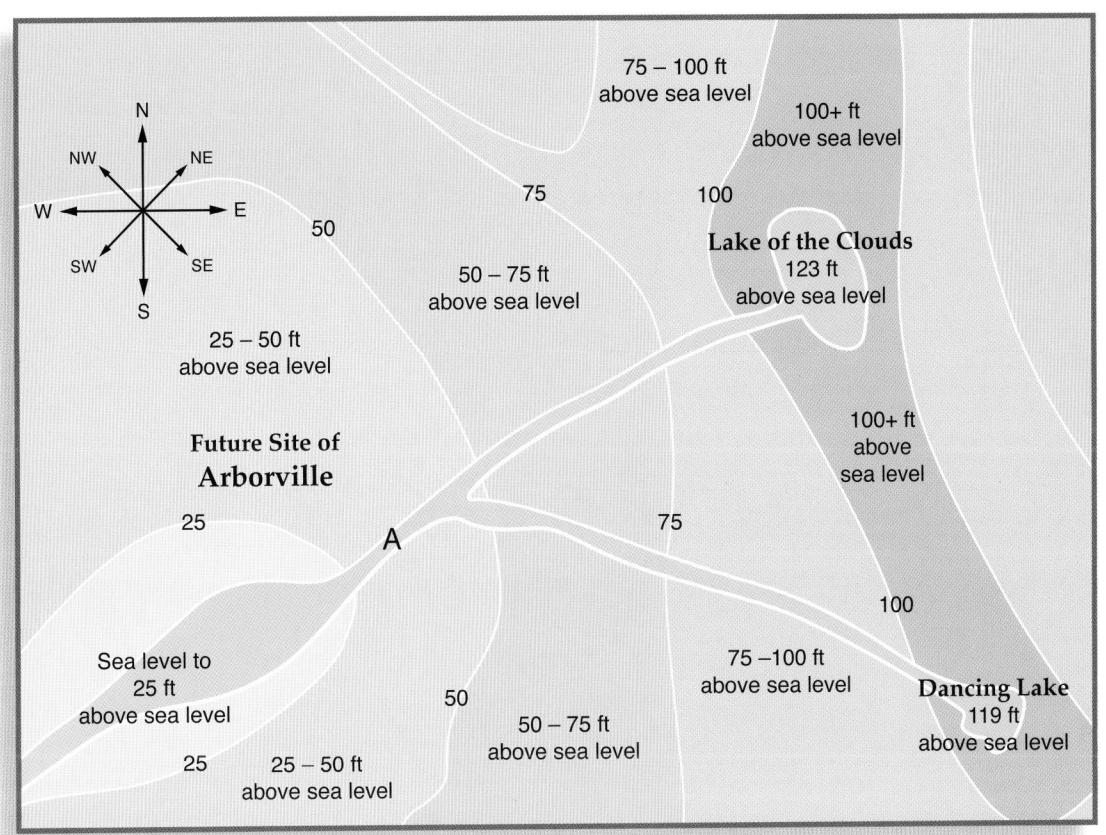

This topographic map shows the area that would become Arborville.

You can see from this topographic map of Arborville that the land sloped down from the northeast (the upper right-hand corner of the map). Lake of the Clouds and Dancing Lake fed two streams. The streams merged to create a river that flowed into the Granflo. Where the two streams converged into a narrow cut (A), there was a strong rush of water with tremendous pressure. In the days of water-powered machinery, water pressure meant power—power to operate things like sawmills.

The First Arborvillians

Felix Sawyer wanted to take advantage of that power. He knew that materials could be floated down river by barge from Arborville to the Granflo, and from there to the city. Supplies could also be floated upstream to his mill if hauled by mules or horses. So he carved a tow path along the north side of the river leading directly to his sawmill (B4). Mules towing barges along the water could walk on the tow path. He also cut lanes through the woods so that felled trees could be easily delivered to his mill. Soon Sawyer realized that he needed a road linking his sawmill with the Granflo, so he built that, too.

The site seemed promising, and other businesses soon followed. Lemuel Arnold opened a granary (C3) to store and distribute the corn and wheat that local farmers were growing. Anthony Sumner opened a general store (B3). Almost everyone kept chickens, but Harry Schechter saw a need for a poultry farm (A4). People in Bay City wanted chickens and eggs, and he could supply

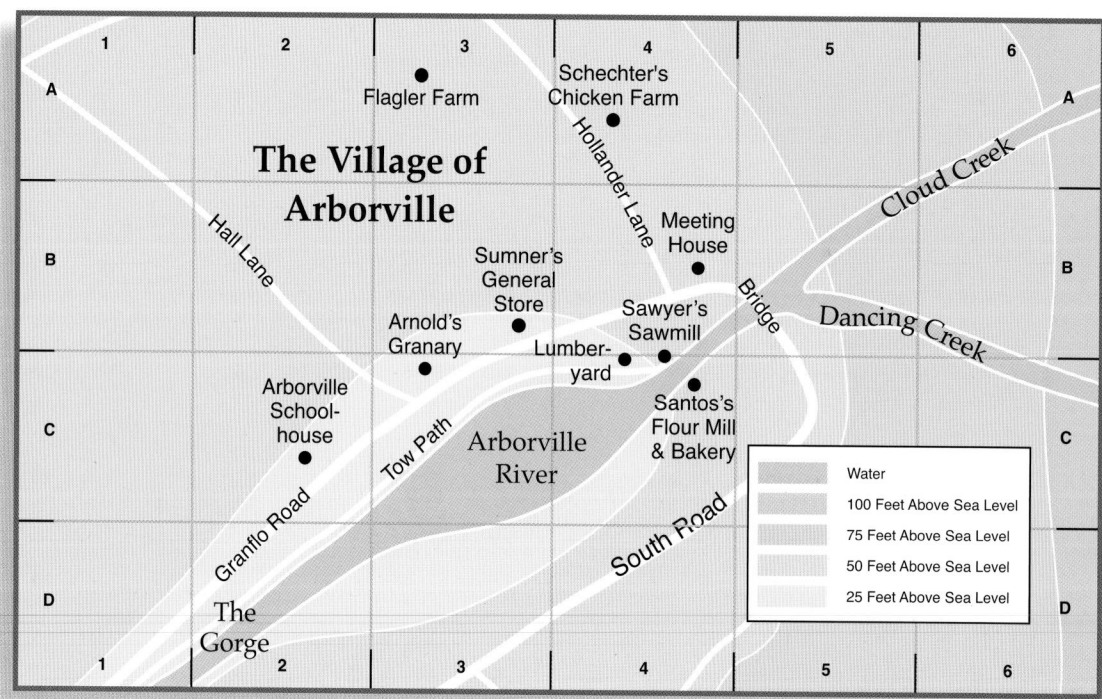

Arborville quickly grew into a thriving village.

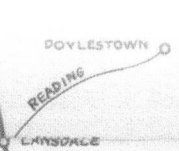

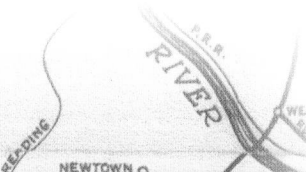

them. Wilbur and Eileen Flagler grew hay, wheat, and corn (A3). They kept a cow in the pasture, and sheep and goats on the hills. A one-room schoolhouse (C2) and a meeting hall (B4) were built as well.

The town built a bridge (B5) across the Arborville River just northeast of Sawyer's mill. This opened up a new area on the left bank for the town to grow. One of the first settlers to take advantage of this new area was Carlos Santos, who opened a flour mill (C4) across the river from the sawmill. His wife, Henrietta, opened a bakery.

	1	2	3	4	5	6	
A	A1	A2	A3	A4	A5	A6	A
B	B1	B2	B3	B4	B5	B6	B
C	C1	C2	C3	C4	C5	C6	C
D	D1	D2	D3	D4	D5	D6	D
	1	2	3	4	5	6	

To find the coordinates B3, find B in the horizontal column, find 3 in the vertical column, and find the box where they meet.

It's easy to locate these sites on the map using the grid coordinates. A grid is simply horizontal and vertical lines labeled with letters and numbers, or coordinates. If you are looking for B3, just find the horizontal row labeled B at the left or right, and the vertical column labeled 3 at the top or bottom. Follow the row and column with your finger until you come to the box that is common to both B and 3. That is the grid coordinate you are looking for.

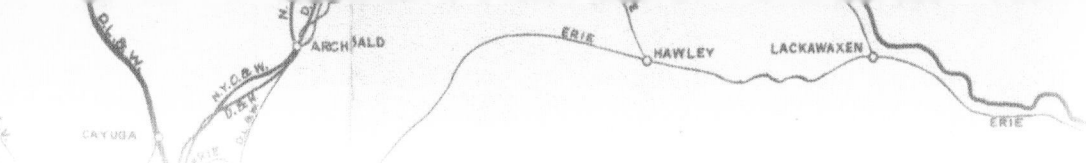

Index

The index above lists places of interest in Arborville. I've used both proper and generic names in the list to make finding things easier. That way, if you have forgotten that the bakery is operated by Henrietta Santos, you can still find it by looking up the word *bakery*.

But just when things were going swimmingly for the folks of Arborville, disaster struck. Here's how one newspaper headline put it.

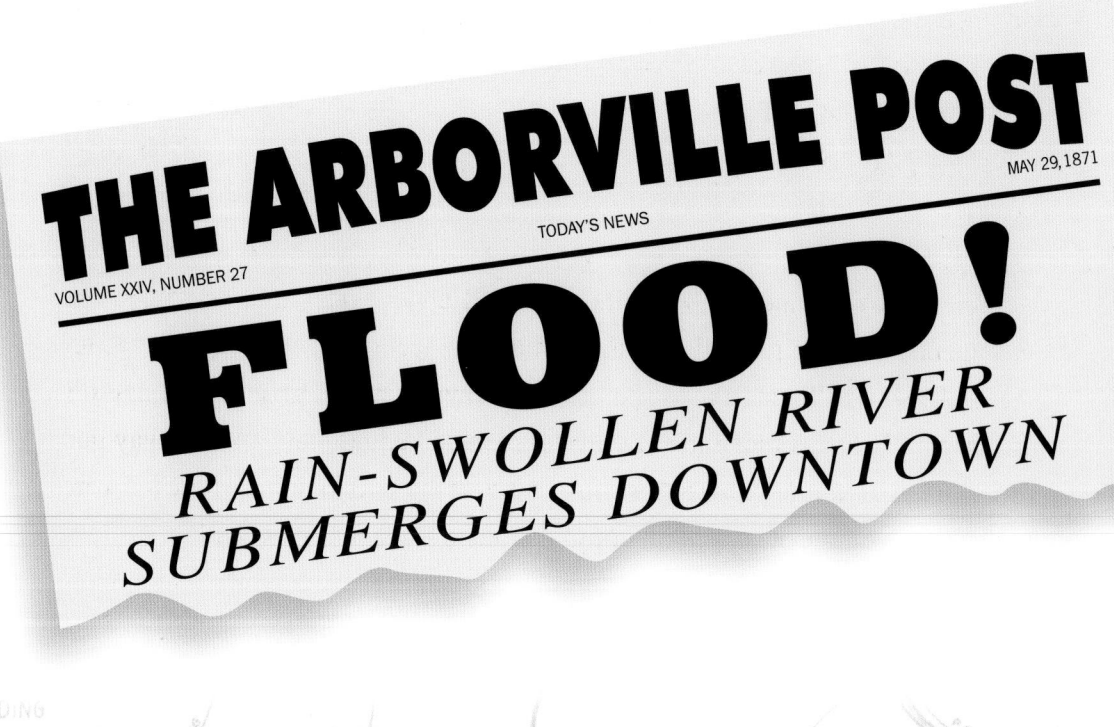

Newspapers called it "The Storm of the Century." The villagers of Arborville called it "our darkest hour." Rain fell for 36 hours, 17 inches of it. It drenched the land. And when the land was soaked and could absorb no more, the runoff created streamlets, and streamlets merged to become streams that found their way down slopes to the creeks that fed the Arborville River and to the river itself.

The swollen river finally overflowed its banks. The roiling waters carried flotsam downstream. Trees—roots and all—were yanked from the earth. Timber and lumber were swept away from the sawmill, and the sawmill itself soon followed. One of the stone piers of the bridge stood fast, but the other gave way, and the bridge itself was washed away.

The debris flowed down to a narrow opening called The Gorge, where it piled up and blocked the flow of water. The debris, jammed against itself, created a natural dam. As a result, the plain in which Arborville stood was flooded. Only the buildings on higher ground were spared—the Meeting House, the Flagler farm, and Schechter's poultry farm all escaped the flood waters.

The map on page 32 shows the water at its highest. Compare it to the map on page 28. You can see that the lakes and creeks are bigger, since they were overflowing their banks. The place where they converged just northeast of the bridge is wider still. The water rose to a height of about 23 feet in Arborville, which you can see. The blue water is just short of the tan that marks the 25-foot height of the land.

The sawmill is gone, but you can see where it was. The general store, Arnold's granary, and the schoolhouse stood under water that first filled the basements, then the main floors, and almost the second floors. When the water receded, Arborvillians found much of their town ruined. The grain in Arnold's granary and the supplies in the general store that had not been swept away had to be thrown out. Soggy schoolbooks were worthless. But the villagers were undaunted. "Our roots are here," said the mayor. "We will rebuild."

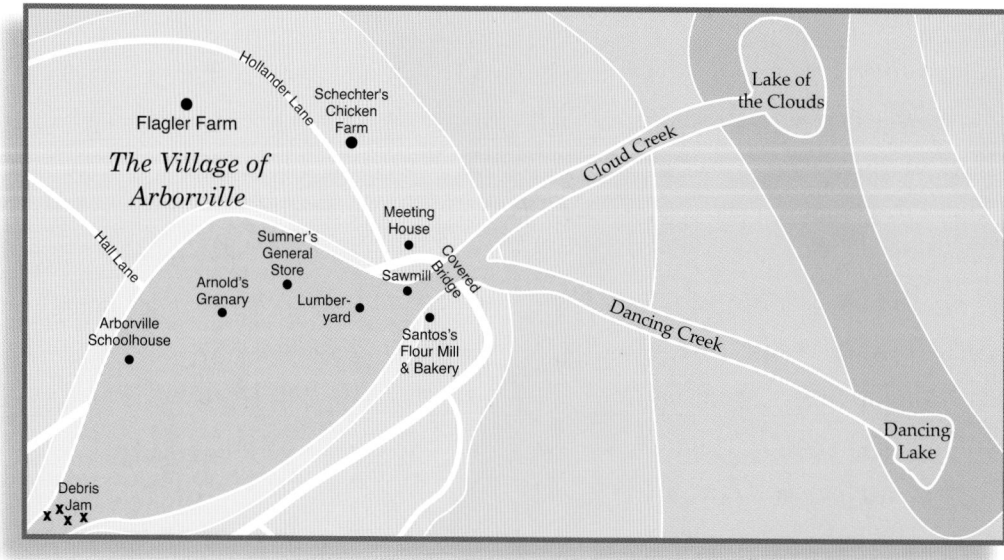

The storm sent water cascading down the hills, filling the streams and river to overflowing.

The Reservoir

And rebuild they did. But the villagers of Arborville did not build their town on the same site. They had learned what nature can do. They built higher. They could afford to because they sold the land that had been their town to Bay City to use for a reservoir.

The flooded plain at Arborville was a little over 30 miles north of Bay City, and it was about 32 feet above sea level. A downward slope or drop of about 15 inches per mile from the reservoir site to Bay City would provide the gravity required for a steady flow of water to the city. Bay City engineers did not have to look any further.

Arborville had a new town, and Bay City had its water supply. Now both towns could grow in earnest.

Making a Topographic Map

You probably already have a pretty good idea of how to make a topographic map, but let's start a new map from scratch anyway. It's good practice. Let's make a topographic map of a small imaginary island that rises rather abruptly from the sea on its eastern shore and slopes gently down to the sea on its western shore. The island is four miles wide at its widest point and seven miles long. The scale we will use is one inch to a mile, or 1" = 1 mile. That means that on our map, the island will be four inches wide and seven inches long.

The first thing to draw is the outline of the island at sea level, which is where the land meets the water. If we were mapping a real island, we might refer to an aerial or satellite photograph for help with the outline. But we're creating this one, so you can make yours any shape you choose. We'll include the bays and inlets, of course.

Let's say that the cliffs on the eastern shore rise to a height of 392 feet. You already know how color can be helpful in showing the height or depth of something. If we show changes in altitude at 50-foot intervals, we will need eight colors to be able to cover a height of 392 feet (from sea level to 50 feet, from 50 feet to 100 feet, and so on). Let's start with light tan for land at sea level, and darken the color gradation the higher we go. If you are drawing this map by hand, remember to increase the pressure on your pencil for each change in altitude in order to deepen the color. You may need to go to a second pencil in the same color family or a different color. When you have made four tones of a tan, for example, go to green and make four increasingly darker tones the higher you go.

Is anything missing? Well, yes! We are creating an island. You know that an island is a body of land surrounded by water, so let's add the water. The land falls away under the water on the eastern shore just as abruptly as it rises out of the water. Likewise, it slopes down just as gradually under the water on its western shore as it rises from it. We used increments of 50 feet of height to show the rise of land. We'll use the same thing to show the depths of the water. If you are drawing this by hand, remember that the harder you press on the blue

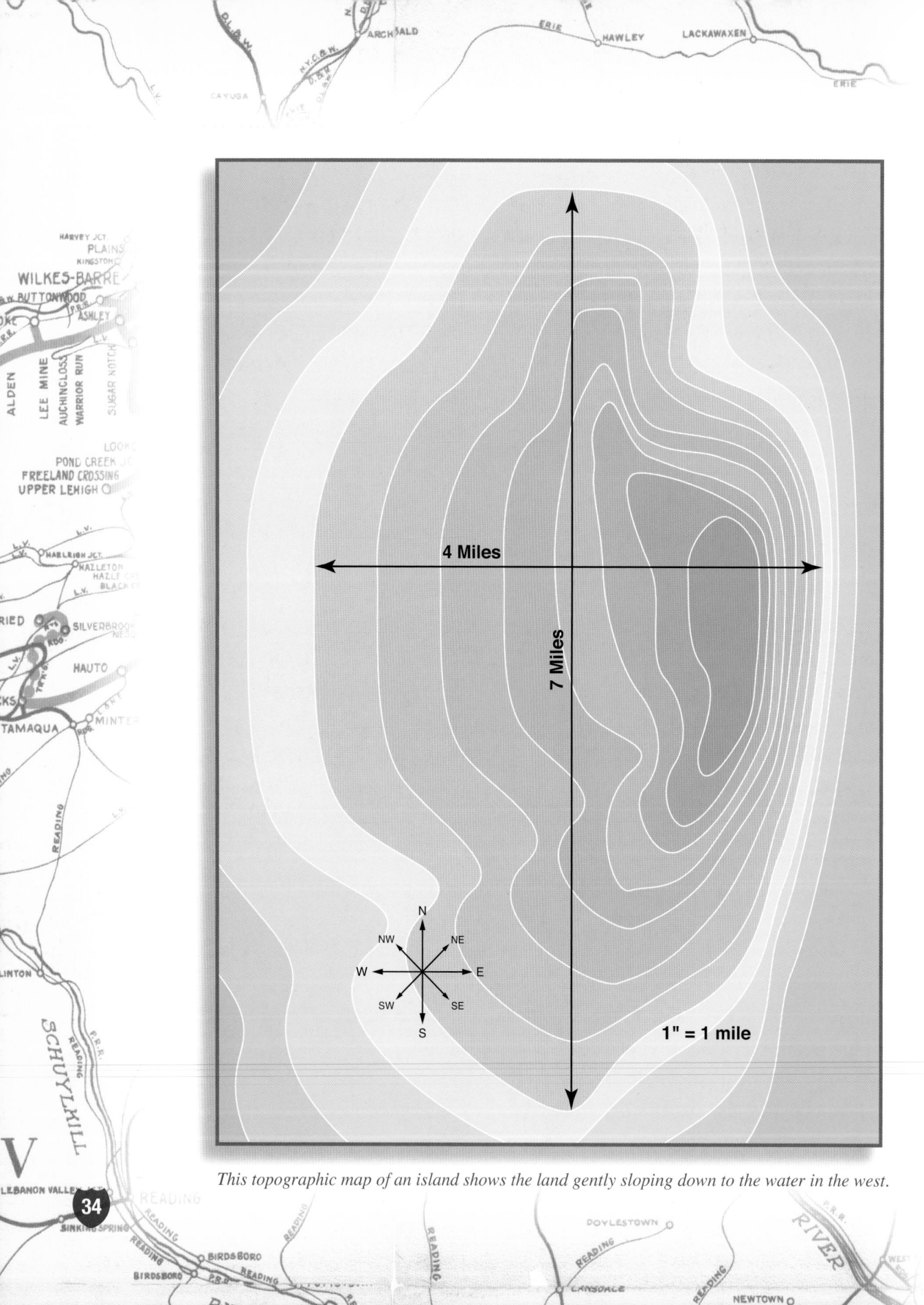

4 Miles

7 Miles

N
NW   NE
W ← → E
SW   SE
S

1" = 1 mile

This topographic map of an island shows the land gently sloping down to the water in the west.

pencil, the deeper the blue.

But don't stop there. You can add other things to a topographic map, such as towns and roads. Perhaps the islanders built a road up the hill on the gently sloping side of the island and then built a resort hotel on top of the cliffs. What else might you show? You have the topography in place. The rest is up to you.

Just one more thing. Instead of an ordinary key, let's do something more interesting. We can use a cutaway diagram of the midpoint of the island, where the cliffs are highest. A 50-foot rise equals $\frac{1}{4}$ inch. It looks like this.

A cut-though diagram provides a sense of the dramatic cliffs in the east.

③ Towns and Cities: Local and Street Maps

Bradford: A Small Town

The map on page 37 shows the small town of Bradford. The town's most famous landmark is a covered bridge that was built in 1862. People come from all over to look at it. The bridge is probably the most photographed object in town. Most photographs are taken from the south shore, where little parks flank Bradford Road. An illustration of the bridge is set in an oval at the top center of the map.

One of the purposes of this map is to boost business and tourism in Bradford, so it shows stores and town buildings. Some are even illustrated, partly because they serve as landmarks and partly because the illustrations add some visual interest to the map. The buildings illustrated are the old railroad station, the town hall, and the Bradford House Bed and Breakfast, Bradford's most famous building. It was built by the man for whom the town is named, Spencer Bradford, an ironmonger who brought the railroad to town. The B&B is operated by Margie Bradford, his great-granddaughter.

Illustrations are fairly common on maps, but road signs are not. They are shown on this map to remind drivers to slow down and drive safely. At the bridge, for instance, you see the official sign for a one-lane bridge. Since the bridge was built in horse-and-buggy days, it is only one lane wide. Drivers have to be patient and courteous. The custom is to have an alternate feed—one car going in one direction, then one in the other.

You can also see railroad tracks. The railroad used to operate passenger trains right through the middle of town. Friday nights were always exciting. That's when workers who had to travel far away to their jobs would return home for the weekend. Families would gather at the station for joyous reunions. But the railroad stopped passenger service years ago, and now the railroad

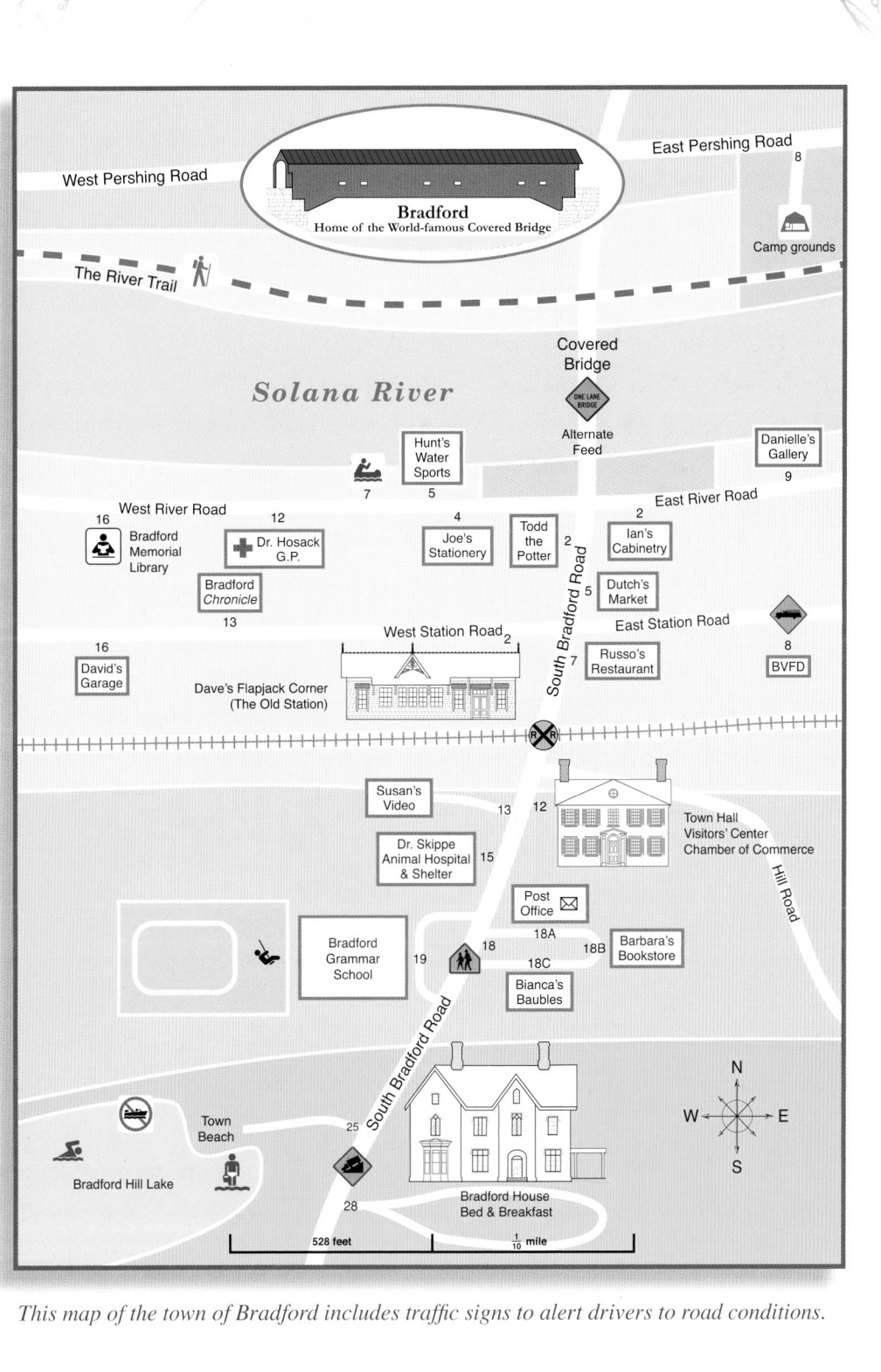

Bradford
Home of the World-famous Covered Bridge

West Pershing Road

East Pershing Road

Camp grounds

8

The River Trail

Solana River

Covered
Bridge

ONE LANE BRIDGE

Alternate
Feed

Hunt's
Water
Sports

7   5

Danielle's
Gallery

9

West River Road

East River Road

16
Bradford
Memorial
Library

12
Dr. Hosack
G.P.

4
Joe's
Stationery

Todd
the
Potter

2

Ian's
Cabinetry

2

South Bradford Road

Bradford
Chronicle

13

Dutch's
Market

West Station Road

2

East Station Road

8

16
David's
Garage

Dave's Flapjack Corner
(The Old Station)

7
Russo's
Restaurant

BVFD

R R

Susan's
Video

13

12

Town Hall
Visitors' Center
Chamber of Commerce

Dr. Skippe
Animal Hospital
& Shelter

15

Hill Road

Post
Office

18A

Bradford
Grammar
School

19

18

18B

18C

Barbara's
Bookstore

Bianca's
Baubles

N

W   E

S

Town
Beach

25

South Bradford Road

Bradford Hill Lake

28

Bradford House
Bed & Breakfast

528 feet

1/10 mile

This map of the town of Bradford includes traffic signs to alert drivers to road conditions.

station is Dave's Flapjack Corner. Dave's pancake recipe was originally his grandmother's.

One freight train still comes through Bradford each day. You can see the official road sign for a railroad crossing. It alerts drivers to slow down, especially since those driving north are going downhill. The map also warns truck drivers about the steep hill, advises drivers about the school zone and firehouse, and so on. The symbols do the talking.

Visitors can take advantage of local attractions such as the camp grounds and hiking trails on the north side of the river, and the canoe and kayak launching site just west of the bridge on the south side of the river. Road signs, which telegraph the subjects in a simple graphic fashion and are well-known to drivers, identify those sites.

A key shows you the scale of things. You can measure distances and figure out how long it will take to get from point A to point B. Most people walk at a pace of about three miles an hour. So if you know that you have one mile to walk, it should take about one-third of an hour, or 20 minutes. You can use a ruler to mark off distances or make your own distance-measuring tool by copying the scale key on the edge of a strip of paper.

The house numbering is measured either north or south from the Solana River on north-south roads, and east or west from Bradford Road on east-west roads. The numbering system is based on tenths of a mile as the crow flies, which means in a straight line. If you are looking for a site on South Bradford Road, line up the tip of your ruler with the south bank of the Solana River and South Bradford Road and measure the distance to the site you are looking for.

An alphabetized list of places of interest serves as a guide. Both individual names and generic names of places are listed, so the generic heading "Restaurants" is followed by an alphabetized list of restaurants.

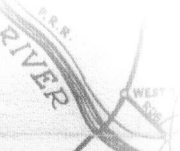

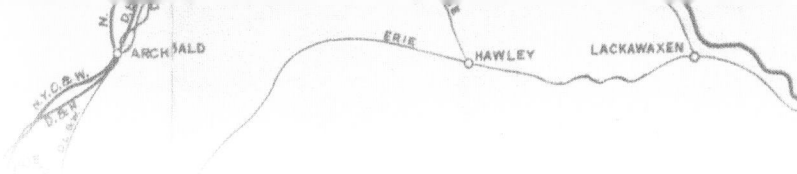

Bradford Places of Interest

Animal Hospital & Shelter, 15 South Bradford Rd

Barbara's Bookstore, 18B South Bradford Rd

Baubles, 18C South Bradford Rd

Bed & Breakfast, 28 South Bradford Rd

Bianca's Baubles, 18C South Bradford Rd

Bookstore, 18B South Bradford Rd

Bradford Chronicle, 13 West Station Rd

Bradford Grammar School, 19 South Bradford Rd

Bradford Hill Lake, 25 South Bradford Rd

Bradford House Bed & Breakfast, 28 South Bradford Rd

Bradford Memorial Library, 16 West River Rd

Bradford Volunteer Fire Department (BVFD), 8 East Station Rd

Camp grounds, 8 East Pershing Rd

Chamber of Commerce, 12 South Bradford Rd

Chronicle, 13 West Station Road

Covered Bridge, spanning the Solana River where South Bradford Rd meets North Bradford Rd

Danielle's Gallery, 9 East River Rd

Dave's Flapjack Corner, 2 West Station Rd

David's Garage, 16 West Station Rd

Dr. Hosack, G.P., 12 West River Rd

Dr. Skippe Animal Hospital & Shelter, 15 South Bradford Rd

Dutch's Market, 5 South Bradford Rd

Fire Department (BVFD), 8 East Station Rd

First Aid, Dr. Hosack, G.P., 12 West River Rd

Flapjack Corner, 2 West Station Rd

Gallery, 9 East River Rd

Garage, 16 West Station Rd

Grammar School, 19 South Bradford Rd

Hunt's Water Sports, 5 West River Rd

Ian's Cabinetry, 2 East River Rd

Joe's Stationery, 4 West River Rd

Lake, 25 South Bradford Rd

Library, 16 West River Rd

Market, 5 South Bradford Rd

Post Office, 18A South Bradford Rd

Pottery, 2 South Bradford Rd

Restaurants

   Bradford House, 28 South Bradford Rd (breakfast, lunch & dinner)

   Dave's Flapjack Corner, 2 West Station Rd (breakfast & lunch)

   Russo's Restaurant, 7 South Bradford Rd (lunch & dinner)

Russo's Restaurant, 7 South Bradford Rd

Susan's Video, 13 South Bradford Rd

Todd the Potter, 2 South Bradford Rd

Town Beach, 25 South Bradford Rd

Town Hall, 12 South Bradford Rd

U. S. Post Office, 18A South Bradford Rd

Video Rental, 13 South Bradford Rd

Visitors' Center, 12 South Bradford Rd

Making a Town Map

The map of Bradford is a map of a picturesque small town. Some of you may live in towns very much like this one. Others of you may live in cities, suburban communities, or towns even smaller than Bradford. No matter which it is, you might like to try mapping all or part of your town or neighborhood. Here's how to do it.

1. Choose an Audience

Who is this map for? Is it for newcomers to town? For a friend to find his way to your home? For a social studies project? Just for fun—for you? Remember, figuring out the audience helps you decide what to include.

2. Plan the Boundaries

Unless your town is really small, you probably won't want to include all of it on your map. So make some decisions about what your boundaries will be. Is there something in your town that's famous, like the bridge in Bradford? If so, you might want to make it the focus or center of your map. On the other hand, your own home might be your focus. A map of your neighborhood would be fun to do, or the neighborhood around your school. Remember, the more you try to include, the smaller your scale will have to be to fit it all on one sheet of paper. You can include much more detail if your map covers a manageable area.

3. Go Out Charting

Get on your bike or, better still, go out charting on foot. This would be fun to do with a partner. Take a pencil, paper, your magnetic compass, and a clipboard. Walk the area that you want to map (or, if you can, find an adult willing to drive you around slowly enough to make the notes you need). Note things like which streets are more important than others (they can be wider on your map than less important streets); which landmarks would be good to include; bridges; creeks; stops for public transportation; shops; restaurants; parks—anything that seems worth showing. It's possible that two different people could map the exact same area and create two entirely different maps (although obviously, certain things would be identical). It depends on the audience and the purpose of the map.

4. Determining Scale

You can make a decision whether or not you want your map to reflect the size of the area you are mapping in perfect scale. Again, a car and helpful driver might come in handy here—the trip mileage indicator can record the distances, and you can reduce them to a scale that works. But don't forget that it's perfectly fine for maps to just give the *appearance* of geographic accuracy. You don't always need an exact scale. Just make your distances relative. If you know it's twice as far from your house to Ruben's house as it is from Ruben's house to the park, your map should reflect that.

5. Make a Rough Draft

Draft your map by hand. Make sure that north is at the top (that's why you took that magnetic compass). Maybe you'd even like to design a compass rose. Start with the streets or roads that are at the outer boundaries of your map, and then fill in the others. Add bodies of water or other natural features, like parks. Then add buildings. Make the draft as complete as you can based on your first charting expedition. You're the only one who has to be able to read this draft, but make it as neat as possible. Then go out again and check to see what you forgot, or what might be in the wrong location. Shift, adjust, and readjust. Do you have names for all the roads? Interesting landmarks? Have you indicated the more important streets? Are any of them one-way? Revise your draft until everything is correct. Draft a map key as well.

6. Learn Some Tricks of the Trade

Read the next section in this book (pages 42–47) for some helpful tips on creating streets. Whether you live in a city with lots of streets or in a small town with just a few of them, the process is the same. Streets are just lines. Some are straight, some curve. You can do it perfectly well either on a computer or by hand, but you might as well learn a few tricks of the trade first.

7. Make Your Final Map

Work either by hand or with a simple computer drawing program, using your revised draft to guide you. Work in the same order as you did in Step 5, starting with the boundaries. What starts out as a final map may end up being another draft, but don't get discouraged. Use color to make your map attractive, keeping in mind that water is blue, and land is usually green or tan. The rest is up to you. The map can include topography if you like (see Chapter 2). You can design an icon (symbol) that is the same for all buildings or you can create different icons for different sorts of buildings. This can be a very personalized map, so have fun with it.

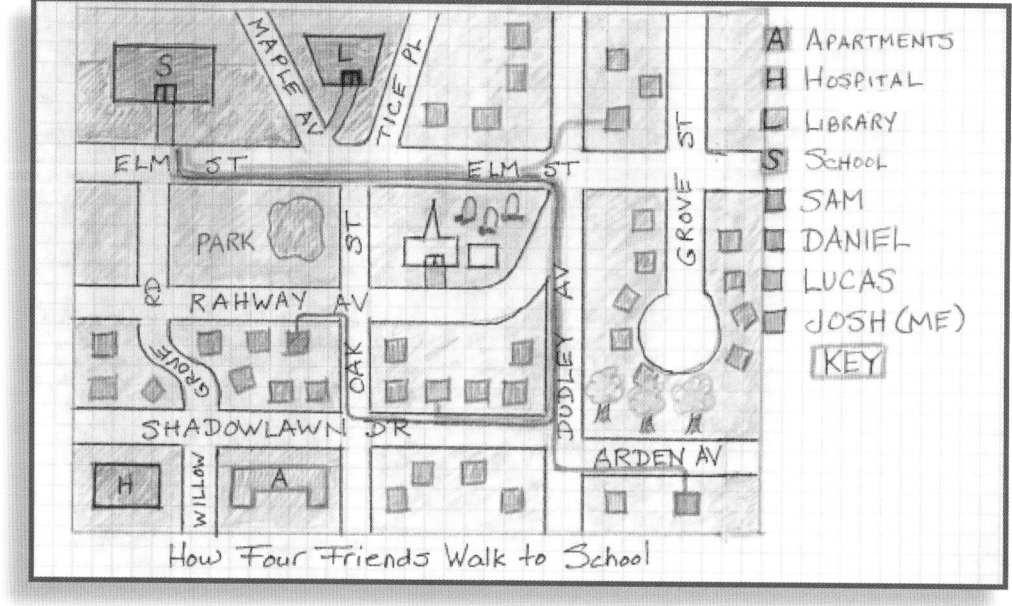

A hand-drawn map showing the routes that four friends take to school.

Making a City Street Map

But maybe you don't live in a town. Maybe you live in a city, and you want to map your neighborhood. No problem! You can make a city street map using what is called a stick map. A stick map is basically lines that represent streets. You have been looking at them in some of the maps of Arborville and Bradford. The lines don't have to be as straight as a stick. They can bend to show curves, but they are still just lines.

Stick maps can be easily made by hand using your tools of the trade, or you may use a computer drawing program, as I have done on the next page. Either way is fine.

You may already know that on a computer, the size of both type and lines is measured in points. The typeface that you are reading now is 12 points.

This type is 9 points.

This type is 18 points.

This type is 24 points.

_____ This line is 1 point thick

_____ This line is 2 points thick

_____ This line is 4 points thick

▬▬▬▬▬▬▬▬▬▬▬ This line is 8 points thick

███████████ This line is 16 points thick

On a computer, draw a rectangle with a light brown outline and white fill. Start drawing gray lines that are two points wide. Place the text alongside the lines. (Text on top of lines is difficult to read.) Court Street on this map has an extra space between *Court* and *Street* to straddle the line for 4th Avenue, and Washington Blvd. has extras spaces as well. If you are making your map by hand, spacing is easier. You can write the letters exactly where you want them. Write lightly at first, even on your final draft, to be sure everything will fit properly.

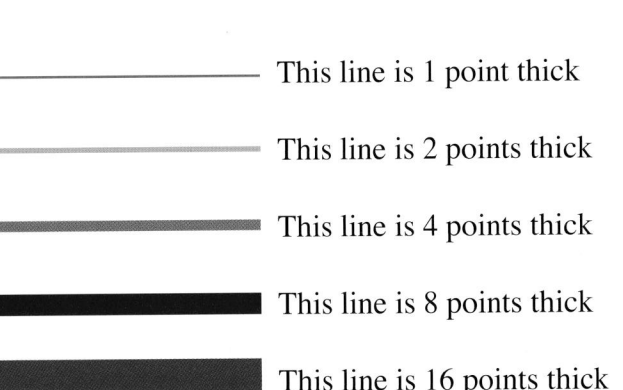

This is the beginning of a basic street map with a white background and gray lines.

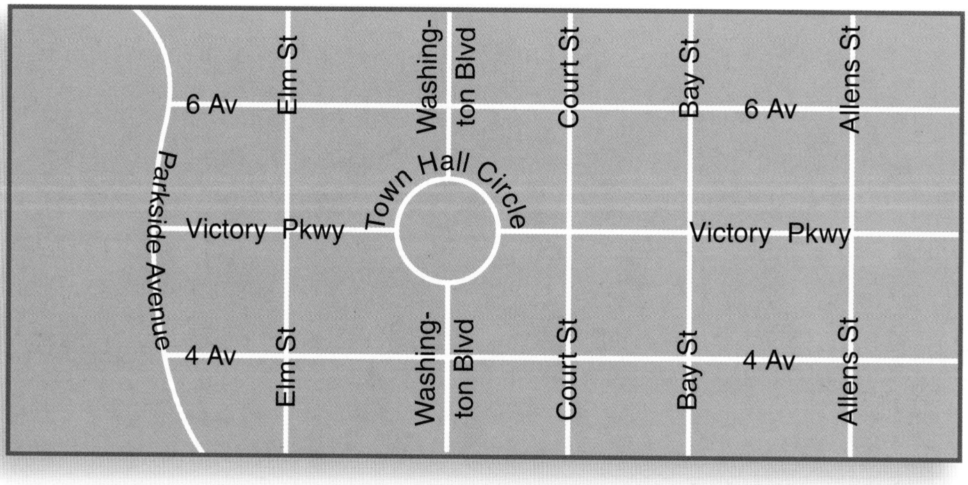

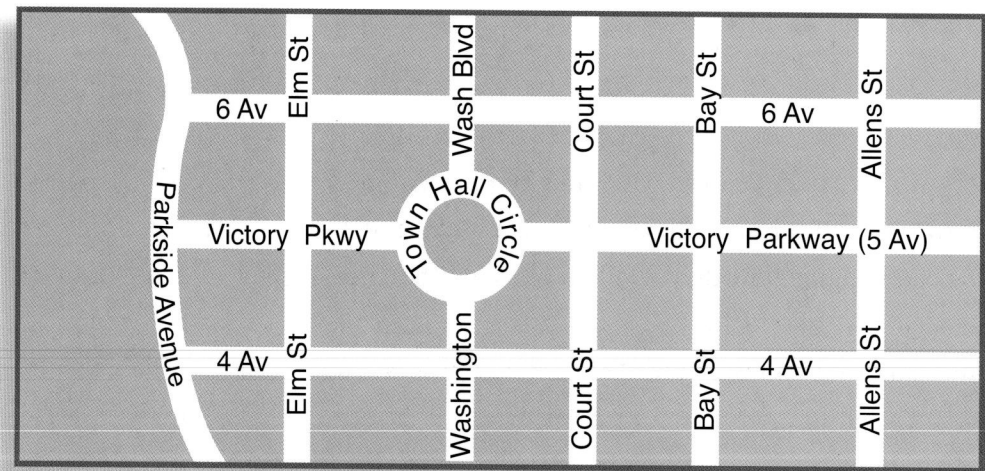

The next step is to make the background gray and the lines white.

Now look at the computerized reverse, or negative image of this map. Where you saw gray, you now find white, and what was white is now gray. Here's how you do this on the computer. Fill the rectangle with gray, and change the lines representing streets from gray to white. Presto! You have a negative image. And you don't have to worry about names straddling streets. You can line them up and center them.

Let's take the same map one step further. Take the same lines on the computer and widen them from 2 points to 11 points. Now the type can sit right on the streets themselves where it belongs, and the street names can be read at a glance (which means more easily).

Now the streets are wide enough to accommodate street names.

By doing this, you have created city blocks without even having to draw them. It's the same drawing, but with just those few changes, the artwork begins to take on the appearance of a real city map. If you are making your map by hand, you do it exactly the same way. Start with lines for the streets. Then widen them by drawing a second line parallel to each line you drew. Erase the lines at intersections and you create blocks with wide streets. Neatly label each street. You can fill in the blocks later with gray or a color of your choice. Graph paper is helpful for this sort of project.

We have now made main streets wider and changed the color of the "blocks" by changing the background color from gray to tan.

You can go a step farther. Make some streets wider than others, to show their importance. Instead of 11 points wide, make important streets 14 points wide. The type for important street names can be 13 points instead of 12 points. Lines that are even wider might represent highways, while lines that are narrower can represent alleys. There is no room on this map for highways, but you can imagine how they would look. With the three different widths for three different kinds of streets, we are creating an information hierarchy, from most important to least important. This can be important on a map.

This is just the beginning. You might find that gray is a difficult background color to work with. Black type on a gray background can make a gloomy-looking map. A good background color is light tan, a neutral color that provides good contrast for type printed on top of it. Experiment to find a color you like.

Now you can begin adding information on the blocks themselves, such as landmarks—your school, the park, the Acme Theater—places that mark the land so that the reader can put things in perspective. They can say, "Well, if I am standing here, and the Acme Theater is there, and the school is over there, I must go this way."

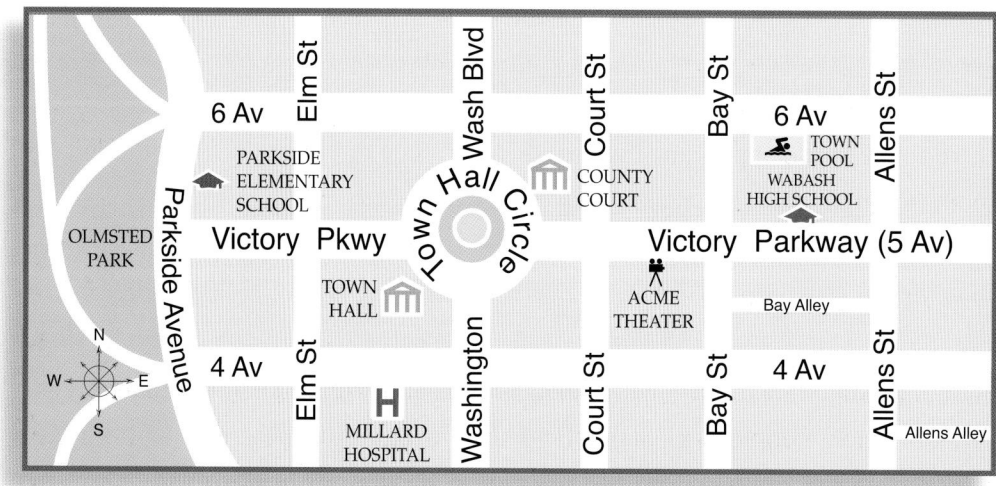

On this map, the icon for schools is a mortarboard.

When you put in places of interest, it can be helpful to use icons to represent different types of places. People think that museums and courthouses have columns, so I've used a simple building icon with columns to represent those places. Movie theaters can be represented by old-style movie cameras, and hospitals by the blue H that you see on road signs. You can find the park on Parkside Avenue, the town pool behind the high school, and a compass rose.

You may have noticed a change of typeface or font on the places of interest labels. The font you are reading now has serifs—little lines on the tops and bottoms of some letters. The font is called Times because it was designed specifically for *The London Times* newspaper. There are hundreds of fonts to choose from. For the places of interest, I used all capital letters (all caps) in a font called Palatino. This is Palatino. It is slightly broader than Times, so it seems larger, even though both are 12 points. An advantage of using all caps is that in almost all fonts, capital letters have no ascenders (like *t*) or descenders (like *y*). NO LETTER IS HIGHER OR LOWER THAN ANY OTHER.

The font I used for street names is a sans serif font, or a typeface without serifs. Sans serif fonts are standard for transportation and street signs, partly because people think they are easier to read. Do you agree? The sans serif typeface chosen for the streets is Helvetica. This is Helvetica. Upper- and lowercase was used rather than all caps because the initial capital letters help guide your eye. Remember, if you are using a computer to make your map and you choose to use upper- and lowercase letters, you have to deal with descenders, such as *y*, which tend to bump into other words or symbols.

If you are making your map by hand, you can still change the sizes of your letters, use both all caps and upper- and lowercase letters, and try out some different lettering styles. It will look just as good. Do you think you need a key to explain that avenues are wider than streets, and streets are wider than alleys? Probably not. People will understand the information hierarchy without any help because it explains itself. That is the secret of good design.

4 Journey by Car: Highway Maps

Creating an Information Hierarchy

Now that you have turned a stick map into a finished street map, you can probably figure out how to make a highway map. You would create a stick map. In this case, however, let's show the roads as dark lines and the land white. With a white background, you can use different colors for different kinds of roads, or highways. This works whether you use a computer or draw the map by hand.

Remember how you prioritized some information on the street map? You created an information hierarchy by showing some streets wider than others. You can do the same thing with highways.

A highway map should show the difference between limited-access roads and regular roads. A limited-access road is a highway with specific entrances and exits. It is an express road. Some of those roads might be as wide as 16 lanes, so lines representing highways should be wider lines on your map. The other roads are local roads. You can get on and off them wherever you want. Use narrower lines for these roads. Add highway names and numbers, and an early draft of the map might look like this:

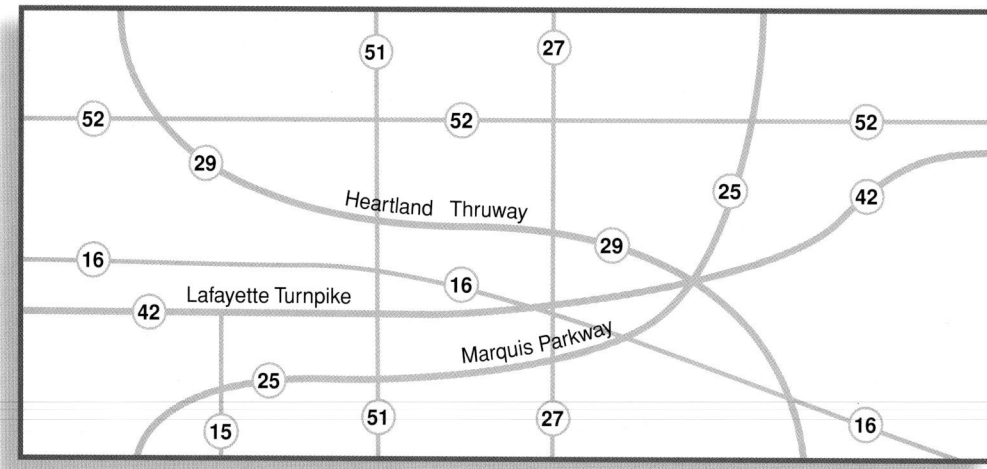

An early draft of a highway map shows highways wider than local roads.

Color-Coding and Road Signs

The map on page 48 is a perfectly good map, but there is a lot more information you can include if you like. There are different kinds of limited-access roads, just as there are different kinds of local roads. The different kinds of roads can be color-coded and have road signs.

On this map, we are going to have the following limited-access roads: an interstate highway; a turnpike, which charges a toll; and a parkway, which allows only passenger vehicles. The two-lane roads, or local roads, will be a federal highway, a state highway, and some county roads.

Limited-access roads should be wide lines, so let's make those lines 3 points ▬▬ , and the other roads 2 points ▬▬ .

We also decided that using different widths is not enough. We're going to use different colors. Not all mapmakers use the same colors to show the same kinds of roads, so choose whatever colors you like. Here are my choices:

Interstate ▬▬   Toll ▬▬   Parkway ▬▬

Federal ▬▬   County ▬▬

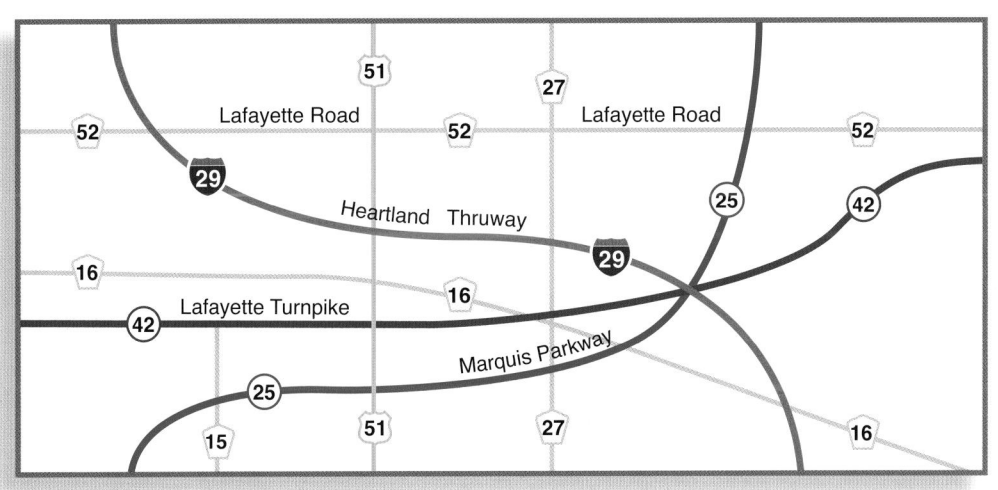

Color-coding the roads and signs makes the map easier to understand.

Try to use symbols on the map that are like the actual signs you see along the roads. If you are drawing your map by hand, you can just copy the shapes and colors. If you are using a computer, you can use highway signs that you find as clip art or on the Internet. The interstates and federal roads have shields (29) (51) . I've used circles or ovals for the state roads (25) and a symbol that resembles a keystone for county roads (27) . And, of course, you need to add names to the roads that have them. Now we're getting somewhere.

Adding More Information

But hang on. We're still missing a few key things, such as junctions, exit numbers, even the names of towns and cities—places where people want to go. Let's start with junctions (where one road joins another). A circle is an appropriate symbol, since there are often traffic circles where you go from one road to another. Let's make the circle white and give it a black border, like this: O. Another symbol might be used to inform the reader where a road terminates, or ends. People often say that when a road ends by bumping into another road, it comes to a T, so I've used a symbol that looks like a T, ⛛.

Limited-access highways have exit numbers that help drivers know when their exit is coming up. I've shown the exit numbers in black boxes with white type. The type is bold for good contrast with the background. Linking the box with the junction symbol is a thin black line called a *leader* because it leads your eye.

Carpooling is good for the environment. Park & Ride sites, where individual drivers can leave their cars in order to carpool with others, are useful on a highway map. On this map, the Park & Ride site is on Route 52 south of Jeanville. The sign you normally see on the highway looks like this: However, when you reduce that sign to fit on this map, it becomes illegible. So I've created a sign that looks like a car in a pool to represent carpooling.

You should have the same kind of information hierarchy on a highway map that you have on a street map. Here I've set county names in 12 point capital letters: MARQUIS. The largest city in Marquis County is Lafayette, which I have set in 12 point upper- and lowercase letters. Gilbert and Jeanville are towns, so they are in 8 point type.

Other subjects can be included, too. Rivers are important, especially since in order to get from one side to the other, you have to go over a bridge or through a tunnel. They may also be also destinations for kayakers, swimmers, and fishermen. Rivers are water, so rivers should be blue.

You can also include major parks, such as state or national parks. Parks are traditionally green. Roads in parks are usually white, but if a highway cuts through a park, it would keep its original color. The highway sign for picnic areas is a tree and a picnic table.

You might even like to include topography on your map. You don't have to draw the hills and mountains to exact scale. Just indicate a bit of elevation so readers will understand where the hills and mountains are. Be sure that the topographic features you include don't interfere with more important information. Remember your purpose. I've used pale gray and indicated the highest point with a darker line.

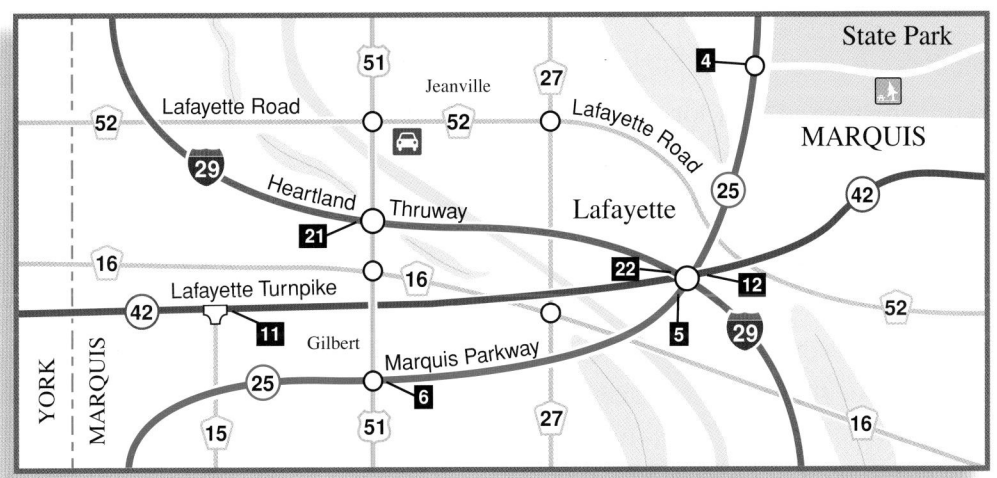

With the addition of a few more details, such as junctions, interchanges and towns, our highway map is now complete.

And there you are. You have just built a highway map. All of the features you've put on the map help put things in perspective for the reader—except for one thing. Where's north?

⑤ Journey by Train: Railroad Maps

Reading a Geographic Railroad Map

Map readers like geographic maps. That's because on these maps, it's easy to see the relationship between one place and another. The geographic railroad map on page 53 is really only one section of a larger map that shows both local and long-distance train service within a 75-mile radius of New York City. Our map is less than a quarter of the entire map. You may not ever make a railroad map such as this one, but it's good to understand how they work.

To help you see distances, concentric rings show the mileage from midtown Manhattan. On this portion of the map, you see only a section of the rings, so they look like arcs. With mileage rings, readers can estimate not just distance, but also time. Many of the stations are for people who commute to and from New York every day, and some people are willing to travel only so far. They might say, for instance, that they will not commute further than 30 miles one way. If so, they can rule out Stamford, Mount Kisco, and Croton-Harmon.

Showing real geography was difficult on this railroad map because the closer to New York City the trains get, the closer together the stations are. There was a lot of squeezing and juggling to make it all fit. But the important thing was to show the relative distances as well as the relationships among stations. In other words, you can't show Station A *south* of Station B if in fact Station A is *north* of Station B.

The local service on this map is operated by the Metro-North Railroad. The southern terminus for Metro-North service is the famous Grand Central Terminal in Manhattan. Metro-North has color-coded its lines: The Hudson Line is green, the Harlem Line is blue, and the New Haven Line is red. Color-coding is also used on the signs in stations, on timetables, and so on.

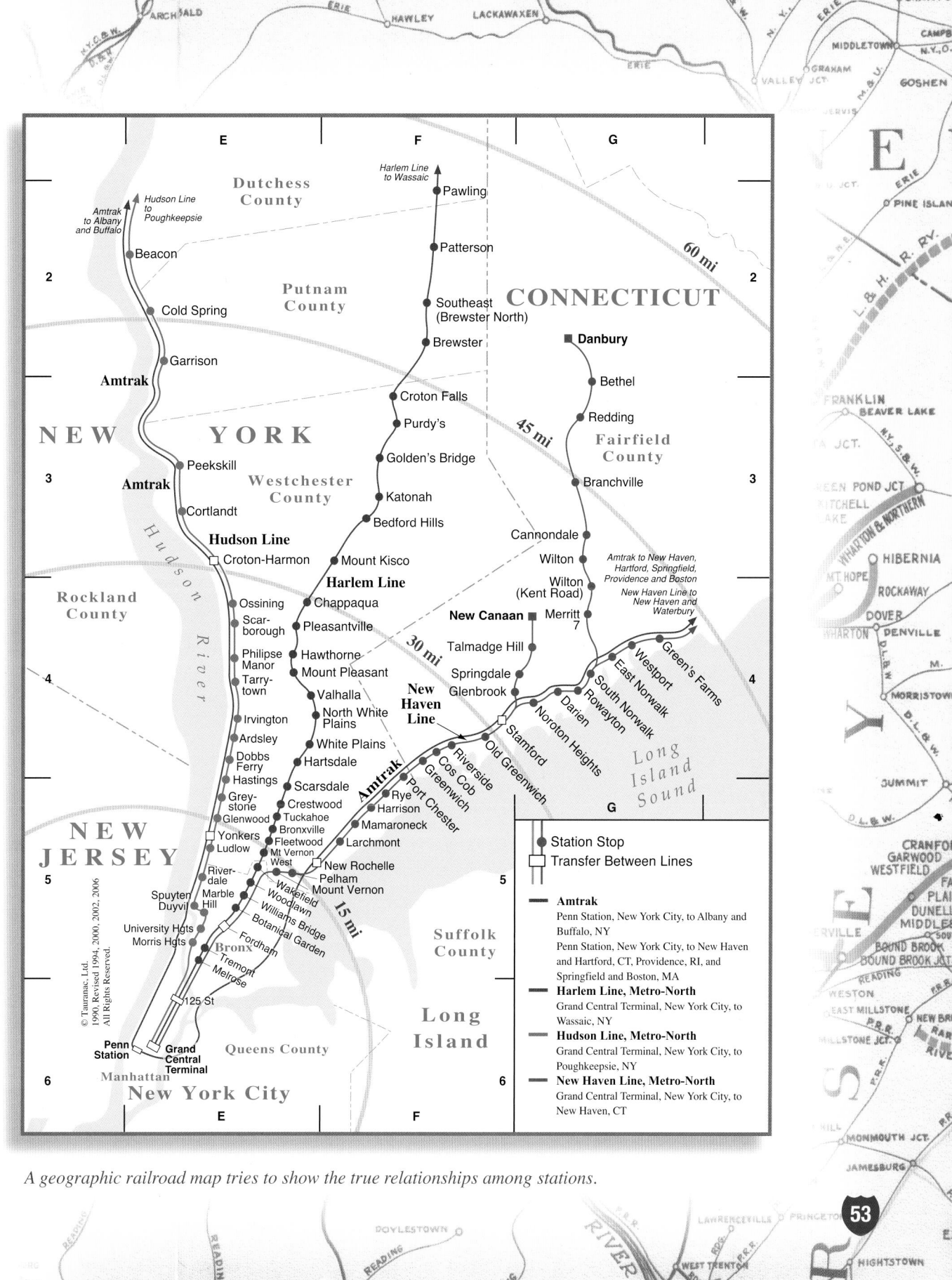

Hudson Line to Poughkeepsie

Amtrak to Albany and Buffalo

Harlem Line to Wassaic

Pawling
Patterson
Southeast (Brewster North)
Brewster
Croton Falls
Purdy's
Golden's Bridge
Katonah
Bedford Hills
Mount Kisco
Chappaqua
Pleasantville
Hawthorne
Mount Pleasant
Valhalla
North White Plains
White Plains
Hartsdale
Scarsdale
Crestwood
Tuckahoe
Bronxville
Fleetwood
Mt Vernon West

Beacon
Cold Spring
Garrison
Amtrak
Peekskill
Amtrak
Cortlandt
Hudson Line
Croton-Harmon
Ossining
Scarborough
Philipse Manor
Tarrytown
Irvington
Ardsley
Dobbs Ferry
Hastings
Greystone
Glenwood
Yonkers
Ludlow
Riverdale
Spuyten Duyvil
Marble Hill
University Hgts
Morris Hgts
Bronx
Tremont
Melrose
125 St

Wakefield
Woodlawn
Williams Bridge
Botanical Garden
Fordham

New Rochelle
Pelham
Mount Vernon
Rye
Harrison
Mamaroneck
Larchmont
Port Chester
Greenwich
Cos Cob
Riverside
Old Greenwich
Stamford

Danbury
Bethel
Redding
Branchville
Cannondale
Wilton
Wilton (Kent Road)
Merritt 7
New Canaan
Talmadge Hill
Springdale
Glenbrook
Noroton Heights
Darien
Rowayton
South Norwalk
East Norwalk
Westport
Green's Farms

Amtrak to New Haven, Hartford, Springfield, Providence and Boston
New Haven Line to New Haven and Waterbury

New Haven Line
Harlem Line
Amtrak

DUTCHESS COUNTY
PUTNAM COUNTY
CONNECTICUT
FAIRFIELD COUNTY
NEW YORK
WESTCHESTER COUNTY
ROCKLAND COUNTY
NEW JERSEY
NEW YORK CITY
Manhattan
Penn Station
Grand Central Terminal
Bronx
Queens County
Suffolk County
Long Island
Long Island Sound

Hudson River

60 mi
45 mi
30 mi
15 mi

© Tauranac, Ltd.
1990, Revised 1994, 2000, 2002, 2006
All Rights Reserved.

● Station Stop
□ Transfer Between Lines

— Amtrak
Penn Station, New York City, to Albany and Buffalo, NY
Penn Station, New York City, to New Haven and Hartford, CT, Providence, RI, and Springfield and Boston, MA
— Harlem Line, Metro-North
Grand Central Terminal, New York City, to Wassaic, NY
— Hudson Line, Metro-North
Grand Central Terminal, New York City, to Poughkeepsie, NY
— New Haven Line, Metro-North
Grand Central Terminal, New York City, to New Haven, CT

A geographic railroad map tries to show the true relationships among stations.

53

The long-distance service on this map is operated by Amtrak. Amtrak does not have an official color-coding system, so purple was selected to contrast with the green, blue, and red. The map on page 55 shows the service north from Pennsylvania Station in Manhattan. The Amtrak service along the west shore of the Hudson River goes north all the way to Albany and Buffalo, New York; to Chicago, Illinois; and to Montreal, in Canada. The Amtrak service that angles northeast along the south shore of New York and Connecticut, travels to Providence, Rhode Island; and Boston, Massachusetts.

Because this map is just a slice of the entire map, you see only the grid coordinates from E – G, 2 – 6. In the index below, each station is followed by a colored dot (or two or three). Those colors identify the railroad lines that stop at that station.

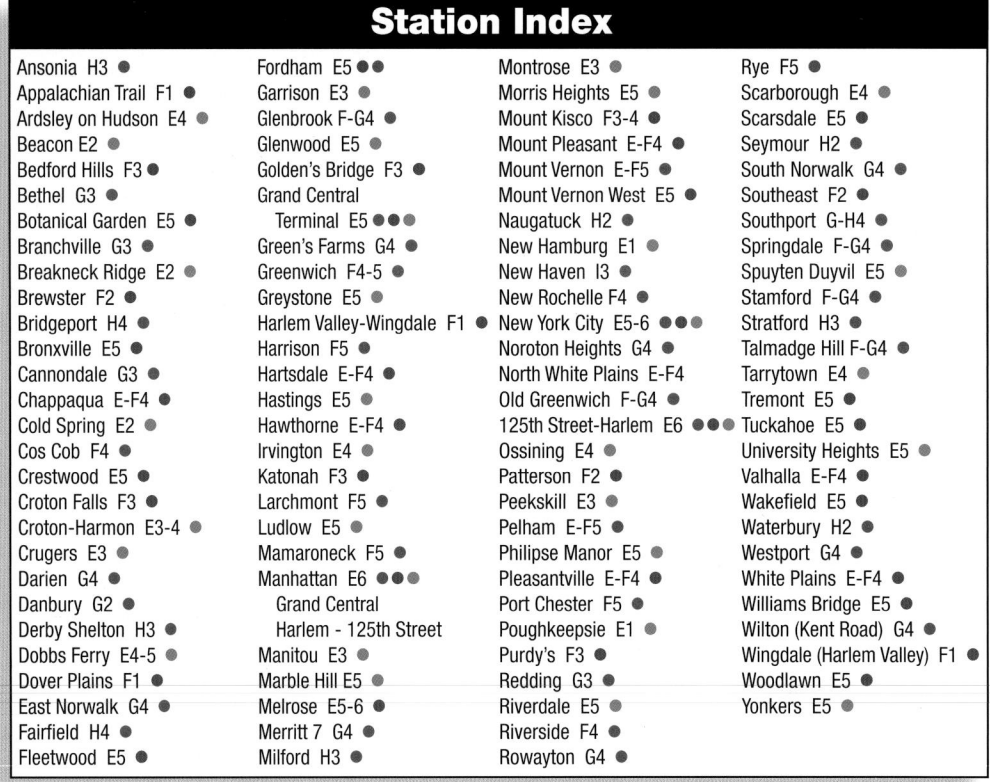

Station Index

Ansonia H3 ●	Fordham E5 ●●	Montrose E3 ●	Rye F5 ●
Appalachian Trail F1 ●	Garrison E3 ●●	Morris Heights E5 ●	Scarborough E4 ●
Ardsley on Hudson E4 ●	Glenbrook F-G4 ●	Mount Kisco F3-4 ●	Scarsdale E5 ●
Beacon E2 ●	Glenwood E5 ●	Mount Pleasant E-F4 ●	Seymour H2 ●
Bedford Hills F3 ●	Golden's Bridge F3 ●	Mount Vernon E-F5 ●	South Norwalk G4 ●
Bethel G3 ●	Grand Central	Mount Vernon West E5 ●	Southeast F2 ●
Botanical Garden E5 ●	Terminal E5 ●●●	Naugatuck H2 ●	Southport G-H4 ●
Branchville G3 ●	Green's Farms G4 ●	New Hamburg E1 ●	Springdale F-G4 ●
Breakneck Ridge E2 ●	Greenwich F4-5 ●	New Haven I3 ●	Spuyten Duyvil E5 ●
Brewster F2 ●	Greystone E5 ●	New Rochelle F4 ●	Stamford F-G4 ●
Bridgeport H4 ●	Harlem Valley-Wingdale F1 ●	New York City E5-6 ●●●	Stratford H3 ●
Bronxville E5 ●	Harrison F5 ●	Noroton Heights G4 ●	Talmadge Hill F-G4 ●
Cannondale G3 ●	Hartsdale E-F4 ●	North White Plains E-F4 ●	Tarrytown E4 ●
Chappaqua E-F4 ●	Hastings E5 ●	Old Greenwich F-G4 ●	Tremont E5 ●
Cold Spring E2 ●	Hawthorne E-F4 ●	125th Street-Harlem E6 ●●●	Tuckahoe E5 ●
Cos Cob F4 ●	Irvington E4 ●	Ossining E4 ●	University Heights E5 ●
Crestwood E5 ●	Katonah F3 ●	Patterson F2 ●	Valhalla E-F4 ●
Croton Falls F3 ●	Larchmont F5 ●	Peekskill E3 ●	Wakefield E5 ●
Croton-Harmon E3-4 ●	Ludlow E5 ●	Pelham E-F5 ●	Waterbury H2 ●
Crugers E3 ●	Mamaroneck F5 ●	Philipse Manor E5 ●	Westport G4 ●
Darien G4 ●	Manhattan E6 ●●●	Pleasantville E-F4 ●	White Plains E-F4 ●
Danbury G2 ●	Grand Central	Port Chester F5 ●	Williams Bridge E5 ●
Derby Shelton H3 ●	Harlem - 125th Street	Poughkeepsie E1 ●	Wilton (Kent Road) G4 ●
Dobbs Ferry E4-5 ●	Manitou E3 ●	Purdy's F3 ●	Wingdale (Harlem Valley) F1 ●
Dover Plains F1 ●	Marble Hill E5 ●	Redding G3 ●	Woodlawn E5 ●
East Norwalk G4 ●	Melrose E5-6 ●	Riverdale E5 ●	Yonkers E5 ●
Fairfield H4 ●	Merritt 7 G4 ●	Riverside F4 ●	
Fleetwood E5 ●	Milford H3 ●	Rowayton G4 ●	

Reading a Schematic Railroad Map

Some people prefer a non-geographic railroad map. For them, the only important information is what station is next, and how many more stations there are until they reach their own. For these commuters, there are schematic maps. You may also see these if you ride the subway in a major city.

There is no real geography on a schematic map. All the stations are the same distance apart. The lines rarely curve gently. The usual angles are 45° , 90° , 135° , or 180° .

The schematic map that follows shows the areas served by Metro-North and Amtrak in the same region as the geographic railroad map on page 53. The tight spacing of the stations allows more stations to be included. In fact, this schematic map shows *all* of Metro-North's service in this area.

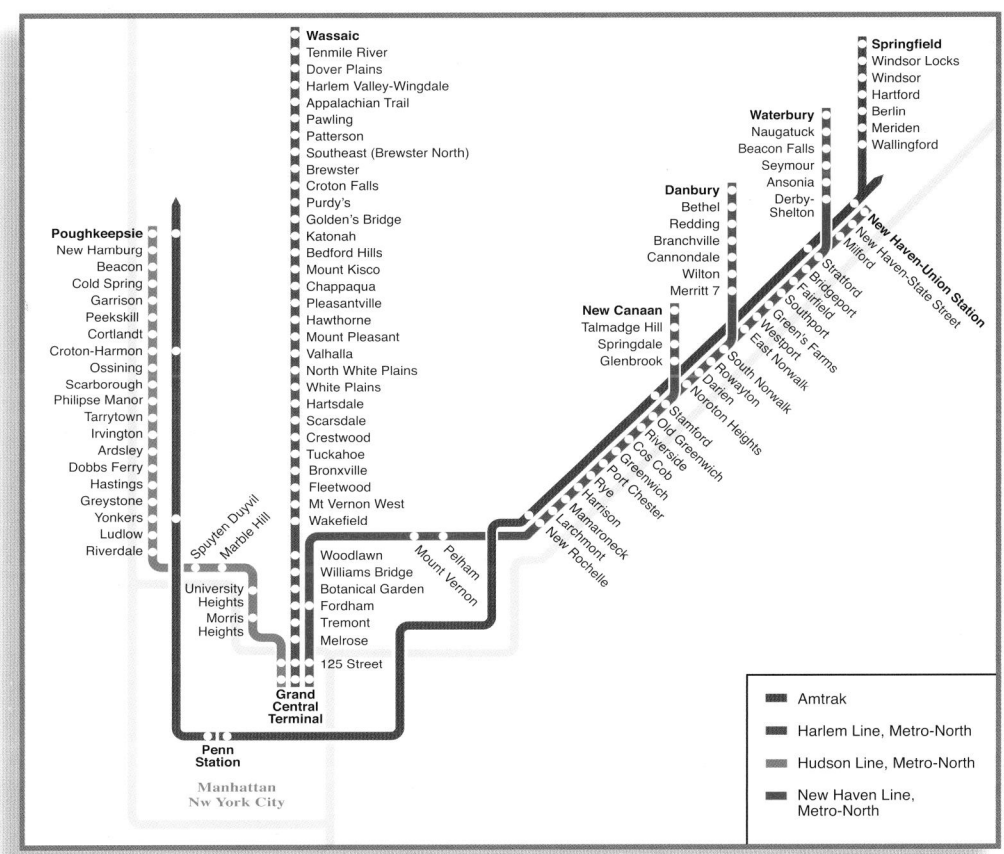

A schematic railroad map does not show true geography.

⑥ Putting It All Together

Reading a Combination Map

Sometimes it's possible to create a schematic map that gives a hint of geographic reality. Here is a section of a metro (subway) map for Washington, D.C. This map shows the heart of downtown Washington where there are many tourist attractions, including the White House, the Washington Monument, the Smithsonian Institution, and the National Gallery. All of the metro stations are in the correct relation to each other, but you can't tell exactly how far apart they are, or how close they are to your final destination.

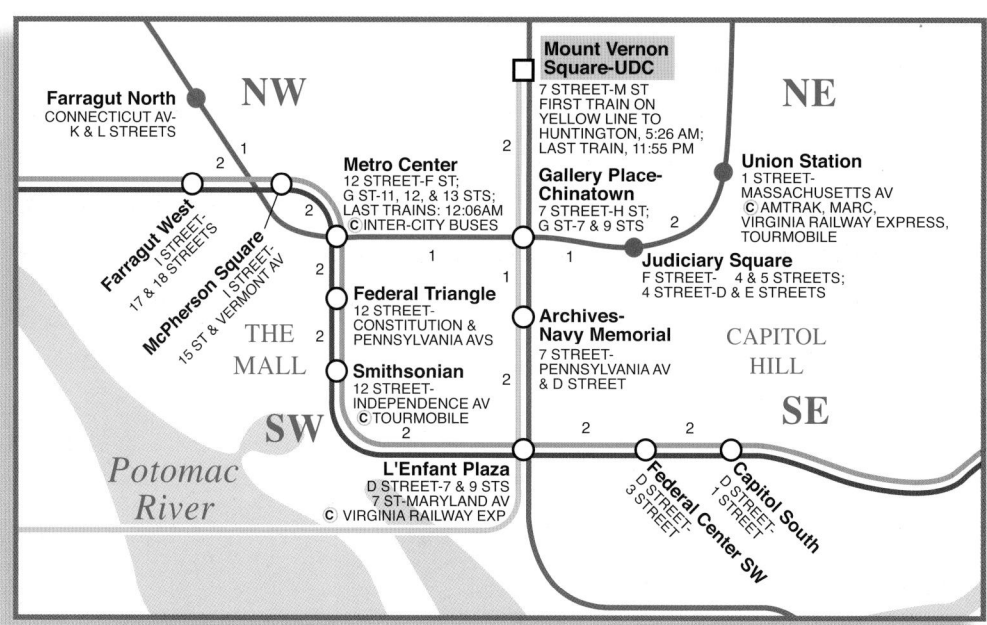

This section of a Washington, D.C., metro map shows the heart of the tourist district.

Nevertheless, unlike either of the railroad maps, there is more information than just station names on this map. For example, you can find the names of the streets on which you will find the metro stations. To a first-time visitor to Washington, the Federal Triangle might not mean much. But under that station name is information that tells you that the entrance is on 12th Street between

Pennsylvania and Constitution Avenues. That's helpful.

You also learn that you can catch the Tourmobile (for a sightseeing tour) at the Smithsonian station. At Metro Center, you can catch inter-city buses. Another feature of this map is neighborhoods, such as Capitol Hill, and major areas of interest, such as The Mall.

The Washington Metro does not operate 24 hours a day, so at termini such as Mount Vernon Square, you are told when the first and last trains depart. Numbers along the routes tell you the running times between stations, so you can figure out how long your trip might take once you're on the train.

Washington D.C. is divided into four geographic segments. The districts are named for compass points: northwest, northeast, southeast, and southwest. In addition to the abbreviations for these district names, the metro map includes dotted lines that separate them. The compass rose at left was tailored for this map.

There's a lot of information on that map. But maybe you'd like even more! On page 58 is a neighborhood map that also shows the metro. The area shown on this map is *exactly* the same area as on the metro map on page 56. It looks entirely different because this map is designed to show various above-ground locations in relation to each other. It's more geographically accurate, so the metro routes are, too.

As the capitol of the United States, Washington D.C. attracts diplomats and tourists from around the world. The map key is in many languages, some of which are shown below. Relative distances are shown in both miles and kilometers for the same reason.

🇺🇸 Street Map		Le Plan des Rues		🏛 Mapa de Calles		Pianta Stradale		Straßenkarte	
Metro Station		**Station de Métro**		**Estación del Metro**		**Stazione della Metro**		**Metro Station**	
Park	NUMBER STREET	Tourist Attraction Open to the Public	RUE ALPHABETISEE	Parc		Site Touristique Ouvert au Public	CALLE NUMERADA	Parque		Atracción Turística Abierta al Público	STRADE A NUMERI	Parco		Attrazione Turistica Aperto al Publico	NUMMERN STRAßE	Park		Sehenswür-digkeiten
🇭 Hospital		🇭 Hôpital		🇭 Hospital		🇭 Ospedale		BUCHS-TABEN STRAßE	
LETTER STREET	AVENUE	RUE NUM-EROTEE	AVENUE	CALLE CLAS-IFICADA POR LETRA	AVENUE	STRADE A LETTERE	AVENUE	HAUPT-STRAßE
Tour-mobile	House Number	Tour-mobile	Numéro de Maison	Tour-mobile	Número de Casa	Tour-mobile	Numero Civico	Tour-mobile	Haus-nummer
	Hotel		Hôtel		Hotel		Albergo		Hotel

Because Washington D.C. attracts so many foreign visitors, the map key is in several languages.

This geographic map of Washington D.C. shows the heart of the tourist district from a different perspective than the metro map

© 1993 Tauranac, Ltd. Revised, 2006
All Rights Reserved.

Making a Wayfinding Plan

You've learned to read and create several different kinds of maps and floor plans. Now you are ready to try creating a wayfinding plan. A wayfinding plan is exactly that—it shows readers how to find their way between here and there. (Come to think of it, that's a pretty good description of a map.) What distinguishes a wayfinding plan is that it usually includes directional signs. A plan for the Main Street Railroad Station follows on page 61. You can use it as a model to make a plan for your school, either on a computer or by hand.

Whichever way you do it, making a plan like this requires careful planning and several drafts before you can make the final version. A map done by hand won't look quite as professional as the one on page 61. But if it's clear and accurate, it will be just as useful and maybe even more interesting! Don't be afraid to give it a try.

A sign in the middle of the Main Street Railroad Station that faces north, toward the entrances to the tracks, might look something like this:

← **Beadle St** 🚌 ↙ Ⓜ ↑ **Tracks 1–6** ↱ **Tix & Info** → **Asylum St** 🚌 ✈

The sign is telling you that Beadle Street, where you can catch taxis and buses, is to your left. To your left and down is the Green Line Metro. Ahead are railroad tracks 1 – 6. The arrow with the 180-degree turn ↱ is telling you to turn around and walk in the opposite direction if you are looking for tickets and information. And to your right is Asylum Street, where you can catch taxis and buses, as well as the bus to the airport.

The signs here have white type on a black background. This is called "dropped-out" type, a style that is used to aid the visually impaired. It is easy to do on a computer. Just draw a rectangle and fill it with black. The type inside the rectangle should be white, so pull down the color dialog box and indicate white type. By hand, just draw a rectangle with a black border and white fill, and use black lettering.

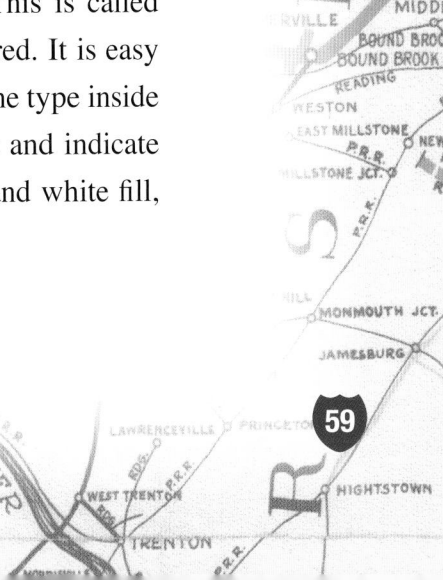

A sign facing south might look like this:

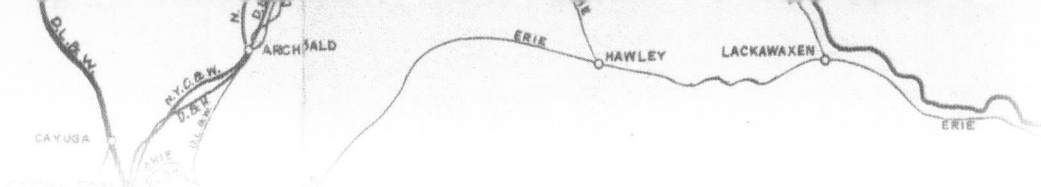

Since you are facing the other way, Asylum Street is now to your left, with taxis, buses, and the airport bus. Straight ahead are Main Street, tickets and information, public toilets, and the Orange Line Metro. To your right and down is the Green Line Metro. And to your right this time is Beadle Street, with taxis and buses.

These signs give you a hint of what you should put on a wayfinding plan for a railroad station: track numbers, the ticket office, streets, transportation, and public toilets. You might also include restaurants and snack bars, stores, and newsstands. Signage in your school might include things like the main office, the principal's office, the library, and restrooms.

Remember the information hierarchy? You need one here, too. Give general information first, then become more specific at decision points. General signage may tell people that toilets are straight ahead. Then comes the decision of which one, so you show both men's and women's rooms. You can see the symbols on the plan. The men's room is on the right as you face it (remember your perspective—we are viewing it upside-down), the women's room on the left. Between them is a baby changing area that both men and women can enter.

Let's assume that this plan is posted in the station. The "You Are Here" arrow indicates where you would be standing if you were looking at it. You would be right under the directional signs that we've already discussed, facing the tracks.

As you can see, the station occupies only one block—Main Street, between Beadle and Asylum Streets. This plan's scale allows us enough room to provide some detailed information. We can show actual bus stops, not just route numbers. We can show the metro platforms, and where transfers can be made from one line to the other. And we can show the entrances to the metro, including those that are handicapped-accessible.

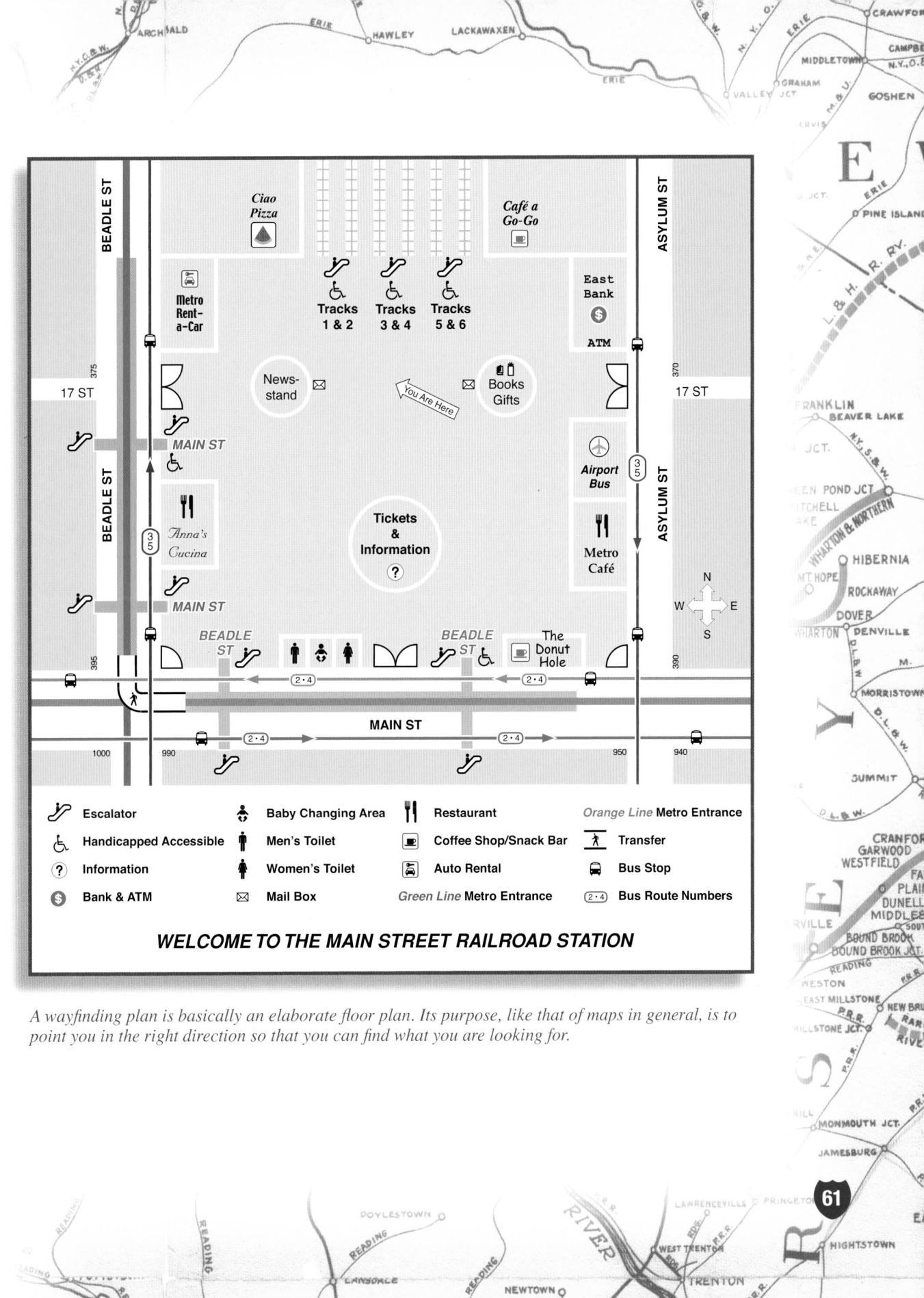

BEADLE ST

Ciao Pizza

Metro Rent-a-Car

17 ST

BEADLE ST

Tracks 1 & 2

Tracks 3 & 4

Tracks 5 & 6

Café a Go-Go

East Bank

ATM

ASYLUM ST

17 ST

News-stand

You Are Here

Books Gifts

Airport Bus

3 5

ASYLUM ST

Anna's Cucina

3 5

Tickets & Information

?

Metro Café

N W E S

BEADLE ST

BEADLE ST

The Donut Hole

2·4

2·4

MAIN ST

2·4

2·4

1000   990   950   940

	Escalator		Baby Changing Area		Restaurant	*Orange Line* Metro Entrance	
	Handicapped Accessible		Men's Toilet		Coffee Shop/Snack Bar		Transfer
?	Information		Women's Toilet		Auto Rental		Bus Stop
$	Bank & ATM	✉	Mail Box	*Green Line* Metro Entrance		2·4	Bus Route Numbers

WELCOME TO THE MAIN STREET RAILROAD STATION

A wayfinding plan is basically an elaborate floor plan. Its purpose, like that of maps in general, is to point you in the right direction so that you can find what you are looking for.

Standard symbols have been used to indicate things like mailboxes, restaurants, and a rent-a-car company. Some, however, have been colorized. Why show a black circle with a dollar sign when you can have a green one, the color of U.S. currency? And, naturally, the airport bus is sky blue. All of these are standard graphics used by the Dept. of Transportation and other agencies. They are available at websites as artwork that you can copy and drop into your map or plan.

Although most of the type is Helvetica (this is Helvetica regular; **this is Helvetica bold**), some fonts on the plan are the same as those used by the shops and restaurants in their logos. This helps them stand out. *Anna's Cucina* is in Nuptial Script. **Metro-Rent-a-Car** is in Techno. *Café a Go-Go* is in Baskerville Italic. *Ciao Pizza* is in *Times New Roman Italic*. I've included Ciao Pizza's slice because that's what they show over their entrance.

To show the entrance that serves each metro line directly, I've set the station names in italic type and colored them to match the color of the line. The streets on which buses operate are in bold type. And since we can see both sides of the streets that border the railroad station, house numbers and entrances and exits to the metro are included there, too.

Everything on the plan is designed to provide guidance for the map reader. But even on a plan of this scale, you can't show everything. It's important to show the entrances to the tracks, the streets, and the metro, but not the entrance to the Metro Café. You never want to clutter up a map with unnecessary information. Do you remember why?

Conclusion

Remember the pirate map we looked at? Pirates like Captain Kidd were usually famous for skills other than mapmaking, but they did make good treasure maps. Captain Kidd's map did three essential things: it showed you where you were, it showed you where places were in relation to each other, and it showed you how to get where you wanted to go. Once you knew that you were in New York City, Captain Kidd showed you exactly how to find Turtle Bay, the two-headed tree, and the rock that reminded him of a Jolly Roger head. Armed with that information, you were able to find the buried treasure. **X** marked the spot.

Captain Kidd stuck to the basics. He did not include information that didn't matter. He included important landmarks, but he didn't show his mate Clive's house, even though he could have. Just because something is in the area you are mapping doesn't mean you have to put it on the map. Was Kidd's map beautiful? Maybe not—but it worked, so it was successful. What's important is that a map be both clear and accurate, which his map certainly was.

The maps you make don't have to look professional. They just have to allow people to orient themselves and then get from one place to another. Remember to make your maps as neat as possible. Use symbols that are easy to read and understand. Write clearly if you are drawing the map by hand. If you are using a computer drawing program, use a type font that is legible. Make everything as plain and simple as you can to serve the purpose of your map. Where Captain Kidd's treasure was buried might have been a mystery, but with his map, the mystery was revealed. That's the essence of mapmaking. Now, if visiting relatives don't know how to get to the local movie theater, it's no problem. You can sit down and create a map that shows exactly where it is in relation to wherever you are. You can include the ice cream parlor if you want—that seems like good information to have on a map of the route to the movies. Go and give it a try. Most of all, have fun.

Glossary

cartographer: a person who makes maps

color gradation: a range of tones or tints of one color that progresses gradually from lightest to darkest, or vice versa

compass rose: a sometimes elaborate design or icon on a map that shows the directions north, south, east, west

concentric rings: circles that grow increasingly larger at a constant rate and share a common center or middle point

coordinates: a set of letters and numbers used to locate a point on a line or surface, such as on a map or globe

cut-away diagram: a drawing of an object rendered as if the object has been sliced open to reveal the inside, which is not normally visible

font: an assortment of sizes and variations of one type style, or typeface

geographic map: a representation of natural and/or man-made features of a place that is drawn to scale

landfill: a system of trash and garbage disposal in which waste is buried between layers of earth to create buildable land

latitude: the angular distance (distance measured as an angle) north or south from the equator to a particular location. The equator has a latitude of 0 degrees. The North Pole has a latitude of 90 degrees North, and the South Pole has a latitude of 90 degrees South.

longitude: the angular distance east or west from the prime meridian—a north-south line that passes through Greenwich, England—to a particular location. Greenwich has a longitude of 0 degrees. The Midway Islands, on the opposite side of the globe, have a longitude of 180 degrees.

meridian: an imaginary circle of longitude that meets at the North and South Poles and connects all places of the same longitude. The prime meridian (0 degrees longitude) passes through Greenwich, England.

peninsula: a body of land that is surrounded on three sides by water

rough draft: the first copy of a piece of writing or a map made up of the writer's original ideas or plans

scale: an explanation of sizes or distances on a map, plan, or model compared to the corresponding actual sizes or distances

schematic map: a non-geographic diagram that shows only specific features

topographic map: a map showing features of the earth's surface, usually with contour lines to show changes in elevation (height and depth)